Progress in IS

Progress in IS encompasses the various areas of Information Systems in theory and practice, presenting cutting-edge advances in the field. It is aimed especially at researchers, doctoral students, and advanced practitioners. The series features both research monographs, edited volumes, and conference proceedings that make substantial contributions to our state of knowledge and handbooks and other edited volumes, in which a team of experts is organized by one or more leading authorities to write individual chapters on various aspects of the topic. Individual volumes in this series are supported by a minimum of two external reviews.

The Series is SCOPUS-indexed.

Melissa K. A. Lukings · Arash Habibi Lashkari ·
Payman Hakimian

Understanding Cybercrime Victim Services

Challenges, Risks, Strategies, and Trends

Springer

Melissa K. A. Lukings
York University
London, ON, Canada

Payman Hakimian
Royal Canadian Mounted Police (RCMP)
Fredericton, NB, Canada

Arash Habibi Lashkari
School of Information Technology
York University
Toronto, ON, Canada

ISSN 2196-8705 ISSN 2196-8713 (electronic)
Progress in IS
ISBN 978-3-032-13272-7 ISBN 978-3-032-13273-4 (eBook)
https://doi.org/10.1007/978-3-032-13273-4

This Springer imprint is published by the registered company Springer Nature Switzerland AG
The registered company address is: Gewerbestrasse 11, 6330 Cham, Switzerland

Competing Interests The authors have no competing interests to declare that are relevant to the content of this manuscript.

Introduction

Cybercrime has become one of the fastest-growing global threats, affecting millions of individuals and organizations each year. According to the FBI Internet Crime Complaint Center (IC3) 2023 report, more than 880,000 complaints were filed in the United States alone, with reported losses exceeding USD 12.5 billion, the highest on record [1]. Similarly, Europol's 2023 Internet Organised Crime Threat Assessment (IOCTA) highlights the increasing sophistication of cyberattacks, particularly in areas such as ransomware, online fraud, and child exploitation [2].

While much academic and policy attention has traditionally focused on offenders and technical defenses, far less emphasis has been placed on the **victims of cybercrime**, their experiences, harms, and access to support. This imbalance has left a critical gap in understanding how victims cope with the consequences of online crime, what services they need, and how institutions can respond effectively.

Victim services encompass a range of assistance programs designed to support individuals who have experienced crime. These services may include legal aid, counseling, support groups, and avenues for compensation. While numerous policies aim to safeguard victims, their effectiveness often falls short. Many victims hesitate to seek help from external agencies, potentially due to barriers such as accessibility issues or ineligibility for certain services. Furthermore, victims frequently report dissatisfaction with the support they receive, stemming from unfulfilled expectations and the inadequacy of trained resources available to meet their needs.

In today's technology-driven world, advancements in digital tools have become integral to our daily lives, enhancing our communication, productivity, and access to information. However, this increased reliance on technology simultaneously exposes individuals and organizations to heightened vulnerabilities. Cybercriminals exploit gaps in our trust and awareness, leading to an alarming rise in cybercrime, including cyberbullying, identity theft, and online harassment.

The emergence of an unregulated online environment has transformed the landscape of crime and victimhood. Governments and businesses are not immune; they face significant risks, including data breaches and substantial financial losses. For instance, the cyberattack on the city of Stratford, Ontario, which rendered its public services inoperable for 12 days, highlights the urgent need for effective response protocols. Despite the growing prevalence of cyberattacks, existing research reveals a notable lack of structured processes and resources to support victims, particularly in the aftermath of such incidents. This gap underscores the importance of developing comprehensive victim services tailored to the unique challenges posed by cybercrime.

The primary goal of this project is to analyze cybercrime victim support systems across various countries to understand the dynamics of victimization in the context of cybersecurity. By examining different national approaches, the project aims to identify existing challenges, gaps in services, and policy shortcomings. The outcome will be a proposed framework that outlines key issues and offers strategic solutions to improve victim support in the evolving cybercrime landscape. We will analyze how governmental and organizational entities become targets of cyberattacks, investigate the tactics employed by perpetrators, and review relevant national and international legislation surrounding cybercrime. We aim to develop a robust cybercrime victim service framework that enhances prevention efforts and expedites recovery for affected entities. A deep understanding of victimology, victimization, and its implications in cybercrime is essential.

In the first chapter, we will delve into victimology and victimization, outlining key theories and historical developments. We will also explore the distinctions between these concepts and their applicability to cybercrime, examining how insights from victimology can inform and enhance existing victim services.

The second chapter will focus on the spectrum of traditional crimes and their victims, offering a detailed analysis of common offenses, reporting rates, and treatment within the criminal justice system. We will juxtapose this information with insights on cybercrime and cybercrime victims, evaluating how victim services address these two domains and identifying strengths and weaknesses in their approaches.

In the third chapter, we will examine cyber law and existing legislation governing cybercrime in an international framework. Understanding these laws is crucial for identifying protections available to victims and assessing the effectiveness of current legislative measures.

The fourth chapter will shift focus to the role of cybercriminals, investigating the methods employed to perpetrate cybercrimes and the motivations driving these individuals. This exploration will provide valuable context for understanding the dynamics of cyber victimization.

In the fifth chapter, we will analyze cybercrime at the national level, particularly its impact on governmental entities across various socio-economic contexts. We aim to assess the factors contributing to the likelihood of cyberattacks and their implications for victim services.

The sixth chapter will extend our analysis to international perspectives, studying ten countries that have experienced significant cyberattacks. We will evaluate the effectiveness of their cybercrime victim services and their capacity to prevent future incidents, providing a comparative lens on different socio-economic backgrounds.

In the seventh chapter, we will investigate the cybercrime victim services currently available in Canada, assess their efficacy for individuals and organizations, and identify areas for improvement.

Finally, in the eighth chapter, we will propose a comprehensive victim services package tailored for cybercrime victims. This innovative package will integrate insights from computer science, social science, and practical applications, providing a structured framework for organizations to implement following a cybercrime incident. The proposed package will also include prevention strategies and recommendations for enhancing national cybercrime policies and legislation.

Through this exploration, we aspire to illuminate the complexities of cybercrime victimization and contribute to developing effective victim services responsive to the evolving landscape of cybersecurity threats.

This textbook aims to illuminate the complexities of cybercrime victimization and contribute to developing effective victim services responsive to the evolving landscape of cybersecurity threats. Our overarching goals are multifaceted: first, we seek to increase awareness of the resources and services available to cybercrime victims, ensuring that those affected understand their options for support and recovery. By highlighting existing programs, we hope to facilitate better access to assistance for individuals and organizations alike.

Second, we aim to identify and advise on gaps in service provision and resource availability. By thoroughly analyzing current offerings, we can pinpoint shortcomings that hinder effective support for victims, paving the way for targeted improvements. Additionally, we will compare and contrast victim services across different jurisdictions, evaluating how varying approaches affect outcomes for cybercrime victims. This comparative analysis will offer insights into best practices and innovative solutions that can be widely adopted.

Our recommendations for service improvement will be grounded in evidence gathered throughout the book, aiming to enhance the efficacy and responsiveness of victim services in the face of cyber threats. Furthermore, we seek to raise awareness of the broader societal impacts of cybercrime, fostering a deeper understanding of how these offenses affect individuals, communities, and economies. By addressing these goals, we aspire to contribute to a more informed and proactive response to the challenges posed by cybercrime, ultimately supporting victims in their recovery and enhancing societal resilience against future attacks.

References

1. FBI Internet Crime Complaint Center (IC3). (2024). *Internet Crime Report 2023*. Federal Bureau of Investigation.
2. Europol. (2023). *Internet Organised Crime Threat Assessment (IOCTA)*. European Union Agency for Law Enforcement Cooperation.

Contents

Chapter 1
Understanding Criminology and Victimology

In this first chapter, we will explore the study of criminology, with an emphasis on victimology. It will be through this lens that we will delve into the intersection of victimology and cybercrime, and the evolving landscape of victim services provision for victims of cybercrime.

1.1 Criminology

Criminology is the scientific study of crime, criminals, and the criminal justice system. It examines the causes, consequences, and prevention of crime, as well as the behavior of offenders, societal responses to crime, and the functioning of institutions like police, courts, and correctional systems.

1.1.1 Key Features of Criminology

Criminology is a multifaceted field that seeks to understand crime in all its dimensions, examining its causes, societal impacts, and the systems designed to address it. It combines insights from diverse disciplines to provide a comprehensive understanding of criminal behavior and justice, ultimately aiming to improve societal safety and fairness.

Criminology includes key features such as the study of crime, analysis of criminal behaviour, a focus on society, evaluation of criminal justice systems, and crime prevention and policy initiatives.

The study of crime is a central feature of criminology, focusing on understanding the nature of crime itself. This involves exploring how crime is defined, categorized,

M. K. A. Lukings et al., *Understanding Cybercrime Victim Services*, Progress in IS,
https://doi.org/10.1007/978-3-032-13273-4_1

and measured. Criminologists analyze crime classifications, such as violent, property, and white-collar crimes, and investigate patterns of offending and victimization across different demographics and regions. By studying trends in crime rates and types of offenses, criminology provides a foundation for identifying underlying causes and evaluating the effectiveness of interventions.

Analysis of criminal behavior is another cornerstone of the field. Criminology delves into the reasons why individuals or groups engage in criminal activities, drawing on psychological, social, economic, and environmental perspectives. This analysis includes examining factors such as mental health conditions, socioeconomic disparities, peer influences, and opportunities for crime. Understanding these dynamics allows criminologists to identify risk factors and develop strategies to address the root causes of criminal behavior.

A focus on society is integral to criminology, as crime does not occur in isolation but within the context of societal norms and values. Criminologists study how societies define crime, how laws are created and enforced, and how cultural, political, and economic factors shape perceptions of criminal behavior. This involves examining how societal structures, such as poverty or inequality, contribute to crime and how certain groups may be disproportionately affected by criminal justice practices.

Evaluation of criminal justice systems is a key aspect of criminology, focusing on the effectiveness, fairness, and impact of law enforcement, judicial systems, and correctional practices. Criminologists assess how well these systems achieve their goals of deterrence, rehabilitation, and justice. They also investigate issues such as racial or gender biases, disparities in sentencing, and the effectiveness of rehabilitation programs, offering recommendations for improvement based on empirical evidence.

Crime prevention and policy forms the practical application of criminology, where theories and research inform strategies to prevent crime, rehabilitate offenders, and enhance community safety. Criminologists develop evidence-based policies aimed at reducing crime rates and addressing its root causes. This includes initiatives such as community policing, restorative justice programs, and environmental design strategies to deter criminal activity. By contributing to policy development and implementation, criminology plays a critical role in creating safer and more equitable societies.

Overall, criminology is a dynamic and interdisciplinary field that seeks to understand the complexities of crime and its impact on individuals and society. Through its focus on crime, behavior, society, justice systems, and prevention, criminology provides valuable insights that inform policy and practice, contributing to a more just and secure world.

1.1.2 *Origins and Evolution of Criminology*

Criminology has deep roots in the intellectual movements of the Enlightenment, particularly through the work of thinkers like Cesare Beccaria and Jeremy Bentham. These philosophers challenged traditional punitive systems and advocated for rational, fair, and proportionate approaches to punishment and justice. Beccaria's seminal work, *On Crimes and Punishments*, argued for a legal system based on clear laws and deterrence rather than vengeance. Similarly, Bentham's concept of utilitarianism emphasized that the justice system should aim to achieve the greatest happiness for the greatest number, laying the foundation for modern penological reforms. These ideas marked the beginning of criminology as a systematic inquiry into the nature and purpose of justice.

The nineteenth century witnessed a paradigm shift with the advent of the positivist school, spearheaded by Cesare Lombroso. Lombroso introduced the idea that criminal behavior could be understood through scientific observation and study, focusing on biological determinism. He argued that criminality was an inherited trait and could be identified through physical anomalies, which he described as "atavistic" features. Although later debunked, Lombroso's work was groundbreaking in framing crime as a phenomenon that could be studied empirically, moving the field away from purely moralistic explanations and toward scientific inquiry.

In the twentieth century, criminology underwent another significant transformation as the focus shifted from individual traits to the influence of social structures on crime. Scholars like Émile Durkheim emphasized the role of societal norms and the breakdown of social order, or anomie, in fostering criminal behavior. Robert Merton expanded on Durkheim's theories, proposing his strain theory, which argued that societal pressures to achieve success could lead to deviant behavior when individuals lacked legitimate means to attain their goals. This sociological perspective broadened criminology's scope, examining the interplay between society, culture, and crime.

Today, criminology is a dynamic and multidisciplinary field that integrates insights from sociology, psychology, biology, law, public policy, and more. Modern criminologists explore a wide range of topics, from the biological and psychological predispositions to criminal behavior to the impact of socioeconomic factors and systemic inequalities. Advances in technology and data analysis have also enriched the field, enabling more nuanced studies of crime patterns and the development of evidence-based policies. This evolution reflects criminology's commitment to understanding crime in all its complexity and devising solutions that promote justice and social well-being.

1.1.3 Core Areas of Study in Criminology

Criminology encompasses a diverse range of subfields that collectively seek to understand crime, its causes, its effects on individuals and society, and the systems in place to address it. Each area contributes unique insights, shaping a comprehensive view of criminal behavior and justice.

Theoretical Criminology forms the foundation of the discipline by focusing on the development and analysis of theories that explain the causes and nature of crime. These theories explore a wide spectrum of influences, from individual psychology to societal structures. For instance, strain theory suggests that crime arises when individuals face barriers to achieving socially accepted goals, leading them to pursue alternative, often illegal, means. Similarly, social learning theory posits that criminal behavior is learned through interactions and associations with others. This area is pivotal for providing the conceptual frameworks that guide research and inform policy-making in criminology.

Sociological Criminology delves into the relationship between crime and social structures, examining how factors like poverty, inequality, and cultural norms contribute to criminal behavior. This subfield highlights the role of societal conditions in shaping opportunities and pressures that lead to crime. For example, it explores how marginalized communities may experience higher crime rates due to systemic inequalities and lack of access to resources. Subcultural theories within this area examine how specific groups develop values and norms that deviate from mainstream society, potentially fostering criminal activity.

Psychological Criminology investigates the individual factors influencing criminal behavior, such as personality traits, mental health issues, and cognitive processes. This area seeks to understand how psychological conditions or developmental factors predispose individuals to engage in crime. Studies may focus on traits like impulsivity or aggression, as well as the impact of childhood trauma or mental illnesses. Psychological criminology often informs rehabilitation strategies by addressing the underlying psychological issues that contribute to criminal behavior.

Biological Criminology explores the genetic, neurological, and physiological factors that may predispose individuals to crime. Researchers in this area study how heredity, brain structure, hormonal imbalances, or neurological disorders influence criminal tendencies. While controversial, this perspective has provided valuable insights into understanding violent or impulsive behavior, offering avenues for early intervention and prevention strategies.

Penology focuses on the punishment, correction, and rehabilitation of offenders, examining the effectiveness of various approaches to justice. This area studies the role of prisons, alternative sanctions, and restorative justice practices in addressing crime and reducing recidivism. Penology also evaluates the societal and ethical implications of punitive measures, exploring how systems can balance accountability with the goal of reintegrating offenders into society.

Victimology, a subfield of criminology, shifts the focus to the victims of crime, examining their experiences, needs, and the societal responses to victimization. It seeks to understand the impact of crime on victims, including psychological and social consequences, while advocating for their rights and support. Victimology also explores patterns of victimization and contributes to preventative measures that reduce vulnerability to crime.

Comparative Criminology broadens the scope by studying crime and criminal justice systems across different cultures and countries. This subfield identifies universal patterns in criminal behavior while highlighting the unique social, cultural, and legal factors that influence crime in specific contexts. Comparative studies provide valuable insights for improving justice systems and fostering international collaboration on crime prevention and policy-making.

Environmental Criminology examines the role of physical spaces and environments in shaping crime patterns. This subfield explores theories such as routine activity theory, which suggests that crime occurs when motivated offenders, suitable targets, and a lack of capable guardians converge in the same place. Crime prevention through environmental design (CPTED) is a practical application of this area, focusing on modifying physical environments, such as improving lighting or urban design, to reduce crime opportunities.

Together, these core areas of criminology offer a multidisciplinary approach to understanding crime and justice. By integrating insights from sociology, psychology, biology, law, and other fields, criminology aims to address the complexities of criminal behavior and develop effective strategies for prevention, intervention, and justice reform (Table 1.1).

Table 1.1 Subfields of criminology

Subfield of criminology	Description
Theoretical Criminology	Focuses on developing and analyzing theories about the causes and nature of crime (e.g., strain theory, social learning theory)
Sociological Criminology	Examines the relationship between crime and social structures, including issues like poverty, inequality, and subcultures
Psychological Criminology	Studies individual factors, such as personality, mental health, and cognitive processes, that influence criminal behavior
Biological Criminology	Investigates genetic, neurological, and physiological factors that may predispose individuals to criminal behavior
Penology	Explores punishment, corrections, and rehabilitation of offenders, including the effectiveness of prison systems and alternative sanctions
Victimology	A subfield focusing on victims of crime, their experiences, and societal responses to victimization
Comparative Criminology	Studies crime and criminal justice systems across different cultures and countries to identify universal patterns and unique differences
Environmental Criminology	Examines the impact of physical spaces and environments on crime, including theories like routine activity theory and crime prevention through environmental design (CPTED)

1.1.4 Applications of Criminology

Criminology has a broad range of practical applications that extend beyond theoretical study to directly impact society by addressing crime and its underlying causes. By combining research, analysis, and policy development, criminology provides tools and insights that benefit various sectors, from law enforcement to social justice advocacy.

Crime Prevention is one of the most significant applications of criminology. By utilizing empirical evidence and criminological theories, criminologists design strategies to reduce criminal behavior and victimization. This includes initiatives such as community policing, situational crime prevention, and environmental design improvements to deter potential offenders. For example, strategies like Crime Prevention Through Environmental Design (CPTED) focus on modifying physical spaces, such as installing better lighting or reducing hidden areas, to minimize opportunities for crime. Criminology also informs public awareness campaigns, encouraging individuals and communities to adopt safer practices and reduce their vulnerability to crime.

Policy Development is another critical application, as criminology plays a key role in shaping laws and criminal justice policies. By analyzing crime patterns, societal factors, and offender behavior, criminologists provide evidence-based recommendations to legislators and policymakers. This ensures that laws and policies are effective in addressing crime and its root causes while promoting fairness and justice. For instance, criminological research has influenced policies related to drug use, domestic violence, and juvenile justice by highlighting the importance of prevention, rehabilitation, and restorative practices over punitive approaches.

Law Enforcement agencies benefit greatly from criminology, as it helps police and investigative bodies understand criminal behavior and develop effective strategies to combat it. Criminologists work with law enforcement to analyze crime data, identify patterns, and predict potential criminal activity. This collaboration improves resource allocation and enhances investigative techniques, such as offender profiling and community engagement strategies. Additionally, criminology contributes to training programs that equip officers with skills to handle diverse situations sensitively and effectively, fostering trust between law enforcement and communities.

Corrections and Rehabilitation is another area where criminology has a profound impact. Criminological insights guide the development of programs aimed at rehabilitating offenders and reducing recidivism. This includes designing educational and vocational training, counseling services, and therapeutic interventions tailored to address the specific needs of offenders. By understanding the factors that lead to criminal behavior, such as substance abuse or lack of economic opportunities, criminologists help create pathways for offenders to reintegrate into society successfully, reducing the likelihood of reoffending and promoting public safety.

Social Justice Advocacy is a vital application of criminology, as it addresses systemic inequalities and social issues that contribute to crime and victimization.

Criminologists often advocate for marginalized populations who are disproportionately affected by crime and criminal justice practices, such as racial minorities, women, and economically disadvantaged communities. Their work highlights the need to address root causes of crime, such as poverty, discrimination, and lack of education, through comprehensive social reforms. By advocating for equity and systemic change, criminology contributes to creating fairer and more inclusive societies.

In summary, criminology's practical applications span crime prevention, policy development, law enforcement, corrections, and social justice advocacy. By bridging theory and practice, criminology not only enhances the understanding of crime but also provides tangible solutions that improve public safety, fairness, and overall societal well-being.

1.2 Victimology

Victimology is a specialized field of study within criminology that focuses on understanding the experiences, causes, and impacts of crime from the perspective of the victim. It examines the complex interplay of factors that lead to victimization, the diverse consequences that victims face, and the relationships between victims and offenders. Furthermore, victimology evaluates how society and institutions respond to victims, highlighting areas for reform and improvement. By prioritizing the needs and experiences of victims, the field plays a crucial role in informing policies, developing prevention strategies, and ensuring that victims are supported and empowered within the criminal justice system and beyond.

1.2.1 Origins of Victimology

Victimology emerged in the mid-twentieth century as a subfield of criminology. Early theorists like Benjamin Mendelsohn and Hans von Hentig developed frameworks for understanding victimization, focusing on victim characteristics and behaviors. Over time, the field expanded to include broader perspectives, such as structural inequalities and systemic factors, leading to the development of critical victimology.

1.2.2 Key Features of Victimology

Focus on Victims

Victimology is fundamentally centered on the experiences and perspectives of victims, placing them at the heart of its analysis. Rather than focusing solely on the offender or the crime itself, victimology seeks to understand how and why certain individuals or groups become victims. This includes examining their vulnerabilities, social contexts, and the circumstances surrounding their victimization. By prioritizing the victim's perspective, the field aims to shed light on the multifaceted impacts of crime on their lives, from physical harm to emotional and psychological distress. This victim-centered approach ensures that their needs, rights, and experiences are not overlooked in discussions about crime and justice.

Causes of Victimization

Victimology delves into the causes of victimization, exploring a wide range of factors that may increase an individual's likelihood of becoming a victim. These causes can be broadly categorized into individual behaviors, situational contexts, and structural inequalities. For instance, personal lifestyle choices, such as frequenting certain environments or engaging in specific activities, might increase vulnerability to crime. Situational factors, like being in a high-crime area or a lack of adequate security measures, also play a role. On a broader scale, structural inequalities, such as poverty, systemic discrimination, or societal marginalization, disproportionately expose certain populations to victimization. By identifying these contributing factors, victimology helps to inform prevention strategies and protective measures.

Impacts of Victimization

The impacts of crime on victims are profound and multifaceted, often extending well beyond the immediate aftermath of the event. Victimology examines these consequences in detail, focusing on the physical, emotional, psychological, and financial effects of crime. Physically, victims may suffer injuries or health complications, while emotionally and psychologically, they may experience trauma, anxiety, depression, or post-traumatic stress disorder (PTSD). Financially, the repercussions can include lost income, medical expenses, or the costs of repairing or replacing stolen property. Recognizing the full spectrum of these impacts is essential for developing effective support systems, therapeutic interventions, and legal remedies that address the needs of victims holistically.

Victim-Offender Relationship

A key area of inquiry within victimology is the relationship between victims and offenders. This aspect examines whether victimization was random or targeted and explores the role of any pre-existing relationships or interactions between the parties involved. For instance, crimes like domestic violence, workplace harassment, or online scams often occur within a context of familiarity or established trust. Understanding these dynamics is crucial for identifying patterns of victimization and designing targeted interventions. It also provides insight into the motivations and behaviors of offenders, which can further inform prevention and response strategies.

Societal and Institutional Responses

Victimology evaluates how society, institutions, and the criminal justice system respond to victims of crime. This includes examining societal attitudes, such as the prevalence of victim blaming, which can exacerbate the harm experienced by victims and discourage them from seeking help. Institutional responses, including law enforcement practices, legal protections, and the availability of support services, are also scrutinized to identify gaps or areas for improvement. Victimology advocates for reforms that ensure fair treatment and adequate resources for victims, fostering an environment where their voices are heard and their needs are prioritized.

Policy and Prevention

One of the primary objectives of victimology is to inform policies and practices aimed at reducing victimization and improving outcomes for those affected by crime. By identifying patterns of victimization and analyzing their causes, victimology contributes to the development of prevention strategies, such as community education programs, environmental design interventions, and public safety initiatives. It also plays a critical role in shaping victim support programs, legal protections, and restorative justice practices that prioritize the rights and well-being of victims. Through its focus on both prevention and response, victimology seeks to create a more just and compassionate society that addresses the root causes of crime while empowering and supporting its victims.

Victimology is the subfield of criminology which studies the victims of crime, their experiences, and the social, psychological, and legal responses to their victimization. It examines the causes, consequences, and patterns of victimization, as well as the relationships between victims and offenders, the role of societal structures, and the functioning of the criminal justice system in addressing victim needs.

1.2.3 Applications of Victimology

The applications of victimology extend across various domains, including the criminal justice system, mental health support, crime prevention, and policy advocacy. By integrating insights from sociology, psychology, criminology, law, and public policy, victimology offers a comprehensive framework for addressing victimization. Through its focus on enhancing victim rights, mitigating the impacts of trauma, identifying and reducing risk factors, and advocating for systemic change, victimology serves as a critical tool in building a more equitable and supportive society for those affected by crime.

Some of the focal applications of victimology include:

Criminal Justice

The study of victimology plays a vital role in improving how the criminal justice system addresses the needs and rights of crime victims. By focusing on enhancing victim rights, victimology advocates for fair treatment, equitable compensation, and access to robust support services throughout the justice process. This includes ensuring victims are informed of their rights, providing resources such as counseling and legal aid, and implementing compensation programs for those who have suffered financial losses due to crime. Victimology's insights also guide the development of restorative justice practices, which prioritize the healing of victims and the resolution of harm caused by crime. By integrating victim-centered approaches, the criminal justice system becomes more effective in supporting victims and fostering trust within communities.

Trauma Support

Understanding and addressing the psychological effects of crime is another critical application of victimology. Many victims experience significant trauma, including anxiety, depression, and post-traumatic stress disorder (PTSD). Victimology provides the foundation for trauma-informed care, which recognizes the profound emotional and psychological impact of victimization. By studying the nature and extent of trauma, victimologists help inform therapeutic interventions, support programs, and recovery strategies tailored to the unique needs of victims. This approach not only aids individuals in their healing journey but also emphasizes the importance of creating empathetic and supportive environments in healthcare, law enforcement, and social services.

Crime Prevention

Victimology contributes to crime prevention by identifying risk factors and patterns of victimization. By analyzing who is most at risk and why, victimologists develop strategies aimed at reducing the likelihood of victimization. This includes designing community programs to address vulnerabilities, implementing educational initiatives to promote awareness, and applying environmental design principles to deter crime. For example, insights from victimology might lead to targeted interventions in high-crime neighborhoods or campaigns aimed at reducing behaviors that increase risk. These efforts are crucial for proactively protecting potential victims and minimizing the overall societal impact of crime.

Policy Advocacy

Victimology also plays a pivotal role in promoting social change to address systemic issues contributing to victimization. This involves advocating for policies that tackle root causes such as poverty, inequality, and discrimination, which disproportionately expose certain groups to harm. Victimologists work to influence legislation and public policy by providing evidence-based recommendations that prioritize victim protection, support, and empowerment. This advocacy often extends to addressing societal attitudes, such as victim blaming, and pushing for structural reforms that foster equity and justice. By bridging the gap between research and policy, victimology helps shape a more compassionate and inclusive society.

A Multidisciplinary Approach

Victimology is inherently a multidisciplinary field, drawing on insights from sociology, psychology, law, criminology, and public policy to provide a comprehensive understanding of crime victims' experiences and needs. By integrating diverse perspectives, victimology not only examines the immediate effects of crime but also considers broader social, economic, and cultural factors that influence victimization. This holistic approach enables the development of more effective interventions, policies, and support systems that address the complex realities faced by victims. Through its interdisciplinary nature, victimology ensures that victims' voices are heard and their needs are met in meaningful and transformative ways.

1.2.4 Types of Victimology

Victimology encompasses various approaches, including these four main schools of thought:

Traditional Victimology

Traditional victimology focuses on understanding the individual and situational factors that influence victimization. This approach examines the characteristics of victims, their behaviors, and the circumstances that may make them more susceptible to crime. It considers how factors like age, gender, lifestyle, and location can increase a person's risk of becoming a victim. Additionally, traditional victimology looks at situational dynamics, such as the time, place, and context in which crimes occur, to identify patterns and vulnerabilities. By concentrating on these specific aspects, traditional victimology provides valuable insights into preventing crime and reducing victimization through targeted interventions.

Critical Victimology

Critical victimology delves into the broader social and structural factors that shape patterns of victimization. This approach emphasizes the role of power, inequality, and systemic structures in creating and perpetuating victimization. It questions how societal norms, economic disparities, and institutional biases contribute to certain groups being more vulnerable to crime and less likely to receive justice. For example, critical victimology may explore how marginalized communities experience higher rates of victimization due to systemic racism or economic disadvantage. This perspective aims to challenge the status quo and advocate for social change to address the root causes of inequality and victimization.

Positivist Victimology

Positivist victimology adopts a scientific and empirical approach to studying patterns and risk factors associated with victimization. This perspective relies on data collection, statistical analysis, and evidence-based methods to identify who is most at risk and why. Positivist victimology often focuses on measurable factors, such as crime rates, demographics, and environmental conditions, to establish correlations and causations in victimization. While this approach provides a clear and methodical understanding of victimization patterns, it has been critiqued for sometimes overlooking the broader social and structural influences emphasized by other schools of thought. Nonetheless, positivist victimology remains a valuable tool for developing targeted prevention strategies and informing policy decisions.

Feminist Victimology

Feminist victimology focuses on the intersection of gender and victimization, highlighting issues such as gender-based violence and the systemic oppression of women. This school of thought examines how patriarchal structures, cultural norms, and power imbalances contribute to crimes like domestic violence, sexual assault, and human trafficking. Feminist victimology also critiques traditional victim-blaming attitudes and seeks to empower victims by advocating for gender-sensitive policies and support systems. By addressing the specific challenges faced by women and other gender minorities, this approach aims to create a more equitable and supportive framework for addressing and preventing victimization.

1.2.5 Traditional Victimology

Traditional victimology is the study of victims and the factors that contribute to their victimization, focusing primarily on the individual characteristics of victims and the situational factors surrounding the crime. Unlike critical victimology, which emphasizes social structures and power dynamics, traditional victimology tends to examine victimization on a more personal level, often aiming to identify patterns and behaviors that might make individuals more likely to be victimized.

Key aspects of traditional victimology include:

1. **Victim Typologies:** Traditional victimologists often classify victims into categories based on their behaviors or roles in the event of the crime. These typologies, developed by early theorists like Benjamin Mendelsohn and Hans von Hentig, might include categories such as "innocent victim," "victim with minor guilt," or "victim who is equally guilty." This approach is sometimes criticized for implicitly blaming victims.
2. **Victim-Precipitation Theory:** This theory suggests that in some cases, the victim may have played a role in precipitating the crime, either through behavior, provocation, or other factors. Marvin Wolfgang's study of homicide, for instance, suggested that some victims might have engaged in behavior that escalated the conflict.
3. **Situational Analysis:** Traditional victimology often considers situational factors, such as the location, time, or social setting, in which crimes occur. By

examining these factors, researchers aim to identify patterns that could help in preventing crime or protecting potential victims.

4. **Victim Blame and Risk Reduction:** Traditional victimology has at times been criticized for contributing to victim-blaming by implying that victims could avoid victimization by modifying their behavior. This focus on personal responsibility can overlook broader societal influences on victimization.
5. **Focus on Victim Services:** Traditional victimology has led to developments in support services and rights for victims within the criminal justice system. The emphasis is often on recognizing the victim's suffering and improving resources like compensation, legal assistance, and psychological support.

While traditional victimology has provided a foundation for understanding victimization and enhancing victim support, it is sometimes limited in its focus on individual behaviors without considering larger social contexts, as critical victimology does.

1.2.6 Critical Victimology

Critical victimology is an approach in criminology that focuses on understanding victimization through the lens of power, inequality, and social structures. Unlike traditional victimology, which often centers on individual characteristics of victims and situational factors, critical victimology examines how broader social forces shape who becomes a victim and how society responds to them. This perspective is grounded in critical theories, such as Marxism, feminism, and post-structuralism, which highlight the role of social institutions, economic inequalities, and power relations in influencing patterns of victimization.

Key features of critical victimology include:

1. **Structural Inequalities:** It looks at how structural factors (like class, race, gender, and social status) create vulnerabilities. For example, marginalized groups are often disproportionately affected by violence and exploitation, partially because of their disadvantaged social positions.
2. **Power Relations:** Critical victimology explores how power dynamics shape both the likelihood of becoming a victim and the response of the criminal justice system. Those with more power in society are less likely to be labeled as victims, and they are also less likely to face victimization in certain forms.
3. **Questioning 'Victim' Definitions:** This approach critiques the way societies define and recognize victims. It questions why some individuals and groups are labeled as "worthy" victims who receive sympathy and support, while others are overlooked, blamed, or even criminalized.
4. **State and Institutional Roles:** It examines how the state and institutions, like the police or social services, may contribute to or even exacerbate victimization, especially among marginalized groups. The criminal justice system may sometimes reproduce inequalities by failing to protect these groups or by enforcing policies that are harmful.

By addressing these dimensions, critical victimology aims to highlight the role of social structures and institutional power in shaping patterns of victimization and the experiences of victims.

1.2.7 The Evolution of Critical Victimology

Critical victimology evolved from traditional victimology as scholars began to question and critique the limitations of traditional approaches, particularly their focus on individual behaviors and situational factors without adequately addressing broader social contexts. This shift was part of a larger movement in criminology and sociology where critical theories, such as Marxism, feminism, and post-structuralism, began to challenge the status quo by highlighting the roles of power, inequality, and social structures in shaping people's lives, including patterns of victimization.

Some of the key ways that critical victimology evolved from traditional victimology include:

1. **Critique of Victim Blaming**
   - Traditional victimology often examined the "precipitation" or "provocation" role of victims, meaning it considered whether the victim's actions might have contributed to their victimization. Over time, this approach was criticized for victim-blaming, as it could imply that individuals were responsible for the harm they suffered.
   - Critical victimology emerged as a response, emphasizing that placing blame on victims overlooks larger social conditions that contribute to their vulnerability. It argues that focusing on individual actions obscures the impact of systemic factors like poverty, discrimination, and social inequality.
2. **Shift Towards Structural Explanations**
   - Traditional victimology tended to look at victimization as a largely individual experience, examining specific incidents and personal characteristics. However, as critical theories became more prominent in the social sciences, scholars began to view victimization through the lens of structural inequality and power dynamics.
   - This shift led to critical victimology, which emphasizes that people from marginalized groups (e.g., based on class, race, gender, sexuality) often experience higher levels of victimization due to structural disadvantages rather than just personal vulnerabilities or behaviors.
3. **Influence of Feminism and Social Justice Movements**
   - Feminist criminologists were instrumental in shaping critical victimology by highlighting issues such as domestic violence, sexual assault, and systemic discrimination. They argued that traditional victimology failed to consider how gender power dynamics contribute to certain types of victimization.

- Social justice movements further emphasized that marginalized groups, such as racial minorities, LGBTQ + individuals, and economically disadvantaged populations, face victimization that traditional victimology had not adequately addressed. This focus expanded the scope of victimology to include an examination of systemic oppression and institutional failings.

4. **Reconsideration of "Who Counts" as a Victim**

   - Traditional victimology often focused on individuals who fit conventional or "innocent" victim roles, like victims of random street crime, while overlooking others (e.g., prisoners, sex workers, homeless individuals). This selective focus was questioned by critical victimologists, who argued that all forms of victimization deserve scrutiny, especially those experienced by marginalized groups who might be dismissed or criminalized by society.
   - Critical victimology emerged with the idea that the label of "victim" itself is socially constructed and that power dynamics influence who is granted sympathy and support versus who is stigmatized or ignored.

5. **Integration of State and Institutional Analysis**

   - Traditional victimology primarily focused on interpersonal victimization and often worked within the existing criminal justice system. However, critical victimology began to look at the role of the state and institutions in perpetuating or exacerbating victimization, sometimes through harmful policies or by failing to protect certain groups.
   - This critique stemmed from a recognition that some institutions may be complicit in victimization, whether through neglect, discriminatory practices, or policies that disproportionately harm vulnerable populations. Critical victimologists argue that these systemic issues must be addressed to reduce victimization rates meaningfully.

6. **Pushing for Societal Change**

   - Traditional victimology has traditionally aimed at helping victims within the current system, often focusing on measures like victim compensation, services, or behavior-based crime prevention.
   - Critical victimology, however, emerged with a broader goal: it not only aims to support victims but also to challenge and transform the social structures and power imbalances that create conditions for victimization. It advocates for policies that address root causes, such as poverty, inequality, and discrimination.

In essence, critical victimology developed as an evolution and critique of traditional victimology, broadening the perspective to consider the societal and institutional dimensions of victimization. This evolution allowed victimology to encompass a deeper, more comprehensive view of why certain groups are more vulnerable to victimization and to push for systemic change alongside individual support.

1.2.8 Distinguishing Traditional and Critical Victimology

The main difference between traditional victimology and critical victimology lies in their focus and approach to understanding victimization. While traditional victimology focuses more on individual characteristics and situational factors, critical victimology emphasizes the broader social, structural, and power-related influences on victimization (Table 1.2).

In summary, traditional victimology tends to focus on individual and situational factors in understanding victimization, often within a more neutral or case-specific framework. Critical victimology, on the other hand, is rooted in critical theory, emphasizing social structures, power imbalances, and the need for societal change to address root causes of victimization.

1.2.9 Similarities Between Traditional and Critical Victimology

Traditional victimology and critical victimology may seem distinct, but they do overlap in a few areas. Both fields share a commitment to understanding victimization and enhancing support for victims, and they occasionally converge on certain issues, especially when addressing victim needs and exploring causes of victimization. Here's how these approaches intersect:

1. Shared Focus on Victim Needs

Both traditional and critical victimology advocate for providing support and services to victims, such as counseling, legal aid, and compensation. While traditional victimology often works within existing structures to improve victim services, critical victimology may push for systemic changes to improve access and quality of these services, especially for marginalized groups.

2. Recognizing Patterns in Victimization

Both approaches examine patterns in victimization, although with different focuses. Traditional victimology may analyze patterns to identify common victim profiles or situational risk factors. Critical victimology, on the other hand, may look at how social structures create conditions that lead to certain groups being more vulnerable. By examining these patterns, both can contribute insights that inform prevention strategies.

3. Influence on Policy and Victims' Rights

Traditional victimology has been instrumental in establishing victims' rights within the criminal justice system, such as victim compensation, protective laws, and advocacy programs. Critical victimology often builds on these efforts, seeking to expand victim protections to cover those who are marginalized or overlooked. While their

Table 1.2 Key differences between traditional victimology and critical victimology

Key differences	Traditional victimology	Critical victimology
Focus on Individual vs. Structural Factors	Primarily examines individual traits, behaviors, or situational factors that may increase a person's risk of becoming a victim. It often looks at specific incidents and the victim's role or vulnerability in those events	Focuses on social structures and power dynamics, exploring how systemic issues like inequality, poverty, race, and gender contribute to patterns of victimization. It considers how marginalized groups are often more susceptible to victimization due to structural disadvantages
Role of Power and Inequality	Usually does not explicitly consider power relations or inequalities in society. It often seeks to understand victimization in a neutral, case-by-case manner without questioning underlying societal influences	Emphasizes the role of power relations and inequality, looking at how the criminal justice system and other institutions may perpetuate victimization, especially for marginalized groups. It questions why some groups are systematically more vulnerable and whether the state or institutions contribute to this
Definition and Recognition of Victims	Often focuses on individuals who fit into more conventional definitions of a "victim" and may categorize victims based on perceived guilt or innocence, potentially leading to victim-blaming	Challenges the way society defines "victim" and examines why certain groups or individuals receive more recognition and support as victims while others are ignored or blamed
Approach to Victim Blame and Risk Reduction	May imply that individuals can avoid victimization through behavioral changes or personal responsibility, sometimes leading to victim-blaming attitudes. It often emphasizes risk reduction strategies for potential victims	Opposes victim-blaming and instead points to broader social issues that increase vulnerability, arguing that solutions should address these root causes rather than focusing solely on individual behavior
Policy Implications and Social Change	Has led to victim support services and advocacy within the criminal justice system, such as compensation programs and victim assistance, but without necessarily addressing underlying social inequalities	Aims to inspire social change by highlighting the need for systemic reforms, advocating for policies that reduce inequalities and empower marginalized groups to decrease overall vulnerability to crime

approaches may differ, both contribute to policy discussions on enhancing victims' rights and protections.

4. Understanding Vulnerability

Both fields aim to understand factors that make people vulnerable to victimization, though their focuses differ. Traditional victimology may emphasize individual traits or behaviors, while critical victimology looks at social inequalities. Together, they offer a more comprehensive view by considering both personal risk factors and broader societal influences.

5. Research on Victim Blame

Traditional victimology sometimes touches on the concept of victim blame, especially in discussing risk reduction strategies. Critical victimology critiques this approach and emphasizes societal responsibilities over individual blame. This tension brings awareness to victim-blaming issues and promotes discussions about more compassionate and inclusive approaches to victim support.

6. Prevention Strategies

Both traditional and critical victimology seek ways to prevent victimization. Traditional victimology might recommend strategies focused on individual behavior or environmental design (e.g., situational crime prevention). Critical victimology might propose broader social reforms to address systemic inequalities. Together, they contribute a range of prevention strategies that address both individual and societal aspects of victimization.

In essence, traditional and critical victimology overlap in their dedication to understanding and supporting victims, even if they differ in their methods and focus areas. Their combined perspectives provide a richer and more nuanced understanding of victimization, balancing immediate support for individuals with long-term societal change.

1.2.10 Positivist Victimology

Positivist Victimology is an approach to the study of victimization that seeks to identify patterns, causes, and risk factors of victimization through scientific and empirical methods. It focuses on understanding how individual behaviors, characteristics, and situational factors contribute to the likelihood of becoming a victim of crime.

Key Features of Positivist Victimology:

1. Focus on the Victim's Role:

    Positivist victimology examines how victims' actions, decisions, or attributes might influence their risk of victimization. This includes studying factors like vulnerability, lifestyle, or proximity to offenders.

2. Scientific Approach:

   It employs empirical methods, such as statistical analysis and criminological surveys, to identify patterns and correlations in victimization.

3. Victim Typologies:

   The approach categorizes victims into types based on their relationship to the crime or offender, such as primary, secondary, or tertiary victims. Early work in this area includes contributions by theorists like Hans von Hentig and Benjamin Mendelsohn.

4. Emphasis on Prevention:

   By identifying risk factors, positivist victimology aims to develop strategies to reduce victimization, such as personal safety measures or environmental design changes.

5. Victim-Offender Relationship:

   It explores the interaction between victims and offenders, including cases of victim precipitation, where the victim's actions or behaviors may have inadvertently triggered the crime.

Goals of Positivist Victimology:

1. Identifying Risk Factors:

   To understand what makes certain individuals or groups more likely to become victims of specific crimes.

2. Developing Preventative Measures:

   To create strategies or policies aimed at minimizing risk, such as public awareness campaigns or environmental interventions.

3. Understanding Patterns of Victimization:

   To analyze trends across demographics, locations, and social contexts, informing law enforcement and policy efforts.

4. Classifying Victim Roles:

   To provide a framework for understanding how victims fit into the larger context of crime and its aftermath.

Contributions of Positivist Victimology:

1. Risk Awareness:

   Positivist victimology has enhanced understanding of how personal behaviors and circumstances may influence victimization risk, helping individuals make informed decisions about safety.

2. Crime Prevention:

Insights from this approach have led to practical applications, such as improved neighborhood design (e.g., better lighting, secure building entrances) and targeted policing in high-crime areas.

3. Victim Typologies:

   Early frameworks for classifying victims (e.g., Mendelsohn's typology) have shaped subsequent research and policy discussions.

4. Focus on Data:

   The use of empirical evidence and quantitative analysis has provided a scientific foundation for studying victimization.

Criticisms of Positivist Victimology:

1. Victim-Blaming:

   A major critique is that it can inadvertently shift blame onto victims by emphasizing their behaviors or choices rather than the actions of offenders or systemic issues.

2. Limited Scope:

   Positivist victimology often focuses on interpersonal crimes and may neglect broader social, economic, or cultural factors contributing to victimization.

3. Overemphasis on Individual Factors:

   It can prioritize personal responsibility over structural causes, such as poverty, inequality, or institutional failures.

4. Neglect of Power Dynamics:

   The approach has been criticized for insufficiently addressing power imbalances, such as those related to gender, race, or class, which critical victimology and feminist victimology highlight.

Example Applications:

- Victim Surveys: Studies like the National Crime Victimization Survey (NCVS) use positivist principles to identify trends in victimization across demographics.
- Crime Mapping: Analyzing geographic patterns to determine high-risk areas and factors contributing to victimization.
- Personal Risk Assessments: Public safety campaigns advising individuals on behaviors to reduce personal risk, such as locking doors or avoiding certain areas.

While positivist victimology has been influential in shaping the field of victimology, its limitations have led to the development of alternative approaches, such as critical victimology and feminist victimology, which incorporate broader social and structural factors in understanding victimization.

1.2.10.1 Feminist Victimology

Feminist Victimology is a branch of victimology that examines the ways in which gender and power dynamics influence victimization, with a particular focus on violence against women and marginalized genders. It is rooted in feminist theory and aims to address how patriarchal structures and societal norms contribute to gender-based violence, as well as how the criminal justice system and society respond to such victimization.

Key Features of Feminist Victimology:

- Focus on Gender-Based Violence:

  Feminist victimology primarily addresses forms of violence that disproportionately affect women, such as domestic violence, sexual assault, stalking, and human trafficking. It examines the societal and structural factors that perpetuate these crimes.

- Power and Patriarchy:

  It emphasizes the role of patriarchal systems and power imbalances in shaping patterns of victimization, highlighting how gender inequality creates conditions for abuse and violence.

- Intersectionality:

  Feminist victimology incorporates the concept of intersectionality, recognizing that gender-based victimization often intersects with other forms of oppression, such as race, class, sexuality, and disability.

- Critique of Victim-Blaming:

  Feminist victimology challenges societal attitudes that blame victims for their own victimization, advocating for a shift in focus from victims' behaviors to perpetrators' actions and systemic failures.

- Systemic Critique of Criminal Justice:

  It critiques the criminal justice system's handling of gender-based crimes, including issues like underreporting, victim shaming, lack of sensitivity in investigations, and lenient sentences for offenders.

- Advocacy and Policy Change:

  Feminist victimology seeks to influence policy and legal reforms to better protect victims, support survivors, and hold perpetrators accountable. It also promotes education and awareness campaigns to challenge cultural norms that normalize or excuse violence against women.

Goals of Feminist Victimology:

1. Understanding Causes of Victimization:

Investigate how societal norms, economic dependency, and institutional failures contribute to victimization, particularly for women and marginalized groups.

2. Improving Support Systems:

   Advocate for trauma-informed, survivor-centered approaches in victim services, such as shelters, counseling, and legal aid.

3. Empowering Survivors:

   Promote initiatives that empower survivors to regain control over their lives, challenge stigma, and advocate for systemic change.

4. Prevention and Education:

   Work to prevent gender-based violence through education, community engagement, and challenging cultural attitudes that sustain inequality.

Critiques of Feminist Victimology:

1. Overemphasis on Women:

   Some critics argue that feminist victimology may focus predominantly on women as victims, potentially overlooking male victims or victims from non-binary and LGBTQ + communities.

2. Neglect of Other Factors:

   While emphasizing gender, it may sometimes underplay other factors, such as socioeconomic or situational influences, that also contribute to victimization.

3. Focus on Victimization:

   Critics suggest that focusing on victimization may inadvertently reinforce a narrative of vulnerability rather than resilience and empowerment.

Contributions of Feminist Victimology:

1. Highlighting Gender Inequality:

   Feminist victimology has been instrumental in bringing attention to gender-based violence and its societal roots, making it a key focus for research and policy.

2. Shaping Legal Reforms:

   It has influenced reforms in areas such as sexual violence laws, domestic violence protection orders, and workplace harassment policies.

3. Advancing Victim Support:

   The feminist approach has led to the establishment of specialized support services, such as rape crisis centers, domestic violence shelters, and advocacy programs.

4. Challenging Norms:

   It has played a pivotal role in challenging cultural norms that perpetuate violence, advocating for societal change toward equality and justice.

Feminist victimology has reshaped the way victimization is understood and addressed, emphasizing the need to confront systemic inequalities and create a more just and supportive society for all victims.

Example Applications

Feminist victimology has been applied in various ways to address gender-based violence, improve support for victims, and challenge societal norms that perpetuate inequality. Below are some examples of its practical applications:

Advocacy for Policy and Legal Reforms

Feminist victimology has driven changes in laws and policies to protect victims of gender-based violence and improve justice outcomes.

- Examples:

  Rape Shield Laws: Prohibiting the use of a victim's sexual history in court to undermine their credibility.
  Domestic Violence Acts: Enacting protective legislation, such as restraining orders and laws mandating harsher penalties for domestic abuse.
  Sexual Harassment Legislation: Introducing workplace policies and laws to prevent and address harassment.
  Marital Rape Laws: Advocating for the criminalization of marital rape in jurisdictions where it was previously legal.

Establishment of Support Services

Feminist victimology has led to the development of specialized services for victims of gender-based violence.

- Examples:

  Rape Crisis Centers: Providing counseling, medical support, and advocacy for survivors of sexual assault.
  Domestic Violence Shelters: Offering refuge and assistance to individuals fleeing abusive relationships.
  Hotlines and Helplines: Operating 24/7 support lines for victims to access immediate help and resources.

Public Awareness Campaigns

Feminist victimology informs campaigns aimed at changing societal attitudes and raising awareness about gender-based violence.

- Examples:

#MeToo Movement: Highlighting the prevalence of sexual harassment and assault, encouraging victims to share their stories.
It's On Us Campaign: Promoting bystander intervention to prevent sexual violence, particularly on college campuses.
One Billion Rising: A global movement to end violence against women and promote gender equality.

Education and Prevention Programs

Programs informed by feminist victimology work to educate communities and prevent gender-based violence.

- Examples:

  Consent Education: Implementing school curricula and community workshops to teach the importance of consent.
  Healthy Relationships Programs: Educating young people on recognizing and fostering respectful, non-violent relationships.
  Workplace Training: Establishing sexual harassment and diversity training programs to create safer environments.

Research and Data Collection

Feminist victimology emphasizes the collection of data to understand the scope and nature of gender-based violence and its impact.

- Examples:

  National Surveys on Violence Against Women: Gathering statistics on domestic violence, sexual assault, and stalking to inform policies.
  Intersectional Research: Studying how race, class, sexuality, and other factors intersect with gender to create unique vulnerabilities.
  Survivor-Led Studies: Engaging survivors in research to ensure their voices shape the findings and recommendations.

Transforming Criminal Justice Practices

Feminist victimology advocates for reforms in the criminal justice system to better support victims and reduce retraumatization.

- Examples:

  Trauma-Informed Policing: Training law enforcement to interact with victims sensitively and avoid retraumatization during investigations.
  Victim Advocacy Programs: Assigning advocates to guide victims through the legal process and ensure their voices are heard in court.
  Specialized Courts: Establishing domestic violence or sexual offense courts with trained personnel to handle cases efficiently and empathetically.

Media Representation and Accountability

Feminist victimology challenges how the media portrays victims and offenders to reduce victim-blaming narratives and promote accurate reporting.

- Examples:

  Media Guidelines for Reporting Sexual Violence: Encouraging journalists to use survivor-centered language and avoid sensationalism.
  Campaigns Against Victim-Blaming: Critiquing movies, news, or advertisements that perpetuate harmful stereotypes about victims.

Global Advocacy and Human Rights

Feminist victimology has been central to international movements addressing violence against women as a human rights issue.

- Examples:

  UN Women Campaigns: Promoting global initiatives like "HeForShe" to engage men and boys in combating gender-based violence.
  Convention on the Elimination of All Forms of Discrimination Against Women (CEDAW): Using feminist victimology research to advocate for its implementation.
  Ending Child Marriage: Campaigning to outlaw forced and early marriages, particularly in developing countries.

Feminist victimology continues to evolve, making significant contributions to victim advocacy, legal reforms, and societal transformation. Its applications emphasize the importance of addressing root causes, empowering survivors, and creating systemic change to reduce victimization and support justice.

1.2.11 Other Schools of Thought

In addition to traditional and critical victimology, several other schools of thought in victimology offer diverse perspectives on understanding victimization. These approaches vary in focus, ranging from psychological analysis to ecological considerations. Below are some of the main schools of thought in victimology:

Radical Victimology

Radical victimology examines the influence of economic and political structures in creating and perpetuating victimization. It focuses on class struggles, systemic inequality, and the role of capitalist systems in shaping patterns of crime and victimhood. From this perspective, victimization is viewed as a byproduct of socioeconomic disparities, with powerful institutions often exploiting or neglecting the needs of vulnerable groups. Radical victimology seeks to uncover how these structural factors contribute to the unequal distribution of harm and disadvantage in society.

Building on Marxist theory, radical victimology argues that capitalist systems inherently generate both victims and offenders as part of broader social conflicts. It views crime and victimization as expressions of these deep-rooted inequalities, emphasizing the ways in which economic systems create conditions of deprivation, exclusion, and exploitation. This school of thought highlights how power imbalances enable certain groups to dominate others, further entrenching cycles of victimization.

Despite its insights, radical victimology has faced criticism for its narrow focus on class conflict and economic systems. Critics argue that this approach can overlook other important forms of victimization based on race, gender, sexuality, and other aspects of identity. Additionally, its emphasis on economic determinism may oversimplify the complex and multifaceted nature of victimization, which is influenced by a wide range of individual, situational, and societal factors. Nevertheless, radical victimology remains a valuable lens for understanding the systemic roots of inequality and their impact on crime and victimization.

Victim Precipitation Theory

Victim precipitation theory explores the ways in which victims may inadvertently contribute to their own victimization. This can occur through behaviors, interactions with offenders, or situational factors that influence the dynamics of a crime. The theory seeks to understand whether victims play an active role, such as provoking or instigating a conflict, or a passive role, where certain characteristics or actions make them more susceptible to victimization. By focusing on the interplay between victim and offender, this theory aims to identify patterns and circumstances that lead to criminal events.

A common application of victim precipitation theory is in analyzing violent crimes, such as homicides or assaults, where conflicts or confrontations may have escalated due to the victim's actions. For instance, it examines whether certain words, gestures, or decisions by the victim may have triggered a response from the offender. The theory also considers broader situational factors, such as being in high-risk environments or engaging in risky behaviors, that might increase the likelihood of victimization.

Despite its analytical approach, victim precipitation theory has been widely criticized for its potential to perpetuate victim-blaming attitudes. By emphasizing the victim's role in criminal events, the theory risks overshadowing the offender's responsibility and the structural causes of crime. Critics argue that this perspective neglects systemic issues such as social inequality, poverty, and cultural factors that shape both victimization and offending. While victim precipitation theory provides insights into the dynamics of crime, its application must be balanced with sensitivity to the broader context and the complex realities faced by victims.

Routine Activity Theory

Routine Activity Theory (RAT) posits that victimization occurs when three key elements converge: a motivated offender, a suitable target, and a lack of capable guardianship. This theory emphasizes the role of everyday activities and routines in influencing the likelihood of becoming a victim. By examining how individuals' routines expose them to risk, such as being in isolated areas, leaving valuables unsecured, or engaging in high-risk behaviors, RAT offers a framework for understanding how crime opportunities arise. Unlike theories that focus on the motives of offenders or the characteristics of victims, RAT centers on the situational dynamics that make crime more or less likely to occur.

One of the notable applications of Routine Activity Theory is its influence on crime prevention strategies. The theory has inspired situational crime prevention approaches that seek to reduce opportunities for crime by altering environments and routines. Examples include increasing surveillance through security cameras, improving street lighting to deter offenders, and designing urban spaces to enhance visibility and reduce isolation. These measures aim to reduce the likelihood of the three elements converging, thereby decreasing opportunities for victimization.

While Routine Activity Theory is highly practical and widely used in crime prevention, it has been critiqued for its narrow focus on situational factors. Critics argue that it overlooks broader social contexts, such as systemic inequalities or structural factors, that contribute to victimization. For example, marginalized groups may lack access to effective guardianship due to socioeconomic disparities, making them more vulnerable to crime. By not addressing the root causes of why certain individuals or groups are disproportionately exposed to risk, RAT can sometimes provide a limited understanding of victimization. Despite these critiques, the theory remains a foundational tool in understanding the situational aspects of crime and victimization.

Lifestyle-Exposure Theory

Lifestyle-Exposure Theory explores the relationship between an individual's lifestyle or routine activities and their likelihood of becoming a victim of crime. The theory suggests that certain lifestyles or behaviors, such as frequenting high-crime areas, staying out late at night, or engaging in risky activities, can significantly increase the risk of victimization. By focusing on the choices and behaviors that place individuals in contact with motivated offenders or high-risk environments, the theory seeks to explain patterns of victimization and why some individuals or groups are more frequently targeted than others.

A key characteristic of Lifestyle-Exposure Theory is its emphasis on the non-random nature of victimization. It asserts that victimization is often a result of predictable interactions between individuals' routines and the environments they occupy. For example, individuals who work late shifts, socialize in poorly lit or isolated areas, or regularly travel alone may face higher exposure to potential offenders. This framework has been used to inform crime prevention strategies that promote awareness of personal risk and encourage behaviors aimed at reducing vulnerability, such as avoiding dangerous areas or adopting safety measures.

However, Lifestyle-Exposure Theory has faced criticism for its potential to perpetuate victim-blaming attitudes. By focusing on the choices and actions of victims, the theory risks shifting attention away from the offenders and the broader social structures that contribute to crime. Critics argue that it overlooks systemic issues, such as economic inequality, discrimination, or the lack of community resources, which may limit individuals' ability to avoid risk. While the theory offers valuable insights into patterns of victimization, it must be applied with caution to avoid placing undue responsibility on victims and to ensure that broader societal factors are considered in addressing crime and victimization.

Developmental Victimology

Developmental Victimology focuses on how victimization affects individuals at various stages of their lives, with a particular emphasis on childhood and adolescence. This approach recognizes that victimization during critical developmental periods can have profound and lasting effects on an individual's psychological, emotional, and social well-being. By examining how these experiences shape life trajectories, developmental victimology seeks to understand the unique vulnerabilities and needs of individuals at different ages, offering insights into the long-term consequences of early victimization.

A central characteristic of developmental victimology is its focus on the psychological impacts of victimization. It explores how experiences of abuse, neglect, or other forms of harm during childhood can influence mental health, behavior, and relationships throughout a person's life. This approach is particularly relevant in fields like child protection, where understanding the effects of trauma is essential for designing interventions. Developmental victimology also underpins trauma-informed care, which aims to provide support that acknowledges and addresses the lasting effects of victimization on development and functioning.

Despite its contributions, developmental victimology has faced criticism for its focus on individual psychological factors, which can sometimes overshadow the broader societal and systemic causes of victimization. Critics argue that by concentrating primarily on the personal impacts of victimization, this approach may neglect the structural conditions, such as poverty, inequality, or inadequate social services, that contribute to the prevalence and persistence of victimization. While developmental victimology provides valuable insights into the personal dimensions of victimization, it is essential to integrate this perspective with a broader understanding of societal contexts to create comprehensive solutions for prevention and support.

Ecological Victimology

Ecological Victimology examines victimization within a broader environmental and social context, considering how the physical and social environments in which individuals live influence their risk of becoming victims of crime. This approach emphasizes the role of neighborhoods, communities, and social networks in shaping patterns of victimization. It highlights how factors such as community cohesion, collective efficacy, and neighborhood crime rates contribute to the likelihood of individuals being targeted by offenders. By analyzing the interactions between individuals and their environments, ecological victimology seeks to understand how the characteristics of a place can either increase or decrease the risk of victimization.

A key characteristic of ecological victimology is its focus on the social and physical aspects of the environment, which are believed to significantly impact crime and victimization. For example, areas with high levels of social disorganization, lower community cohesion, or reduced informal social control may experience higher rates of crime and victimization. Conversely, communities with strong social networks, shared norms, and collective action may provide greater protection and lower victimization risks. This approach is particularly valuable for understanding the importance of place and community in shaping individuals' experiences of crime and the support systems available to them.

However, ecological victimology has been criticized for its geographic focus, which can sometimes overlook individual-level factors and broader systemic issues that contribute to victimization. Critics argue that while the neighborhood and community context is important, it should not overshadow the roles of personal behavior, social inequalities, and structural conditions that influence crime. Additionally, the focus on geographic factors may fail to fully account for the complexity of victimization, especially in cases where individual actions or broader societal structures play a more significant role in shaping outcomes. Despite these limitations, ecological victimology offers valuable insights into how environmental and social factors interact to influence victimization and provides a framework for designing community-based crime prevention strategies.

Psychological Victimology

Psychological Victimology focuses on the mental and emotional effects of victimization, particularly how individuals process trauma and the long-term psychological consequences they face. This approach examines the psychological aftermath of crime, exploring how victims cope with stress, fear, and trauma, and how these experiences affect their mental health. Commonly, psychological victimology applies frameworks like Post-Traumatic Stress Disorder (PTSD) to understand how victimization can lead to psychological distress, altering individuals' emotional well-being and cognitive functioning. By delving into these psychological impacts, the field aims to provide a comprehensive understanding of how crime shapes victims beyond the immediate physical effects.

A significant characteristic of psychological victimology is its contribution to trauma-informed care, which seeks to address the psychological needs of victims in a way that acknowledges their trauma and promotes healing. This approach has informed mental health interventions and victim recovery programs, helping to create supportive environments where victims can process their experiences and rebuild their lives. It has also provided valuable insights into therapeutic practices that are tailored to the unique needs of crime victims, ensuring that they receive the mental health care necessary for recovery. Through these contributions, psychological victimology has played a crucial role in improving the support systems available to victims of crime.

However, psychological victimology has faced criticism for its heavy focus on individual-level factors, sometimes overlooking the broader social, structural, and situational conditions that contribute to victimization. Critics argue that by focusing predominantly on the psychological experiences of victims, this approach may fail to address the root causes of crime, such as inequality, social exclusion, and systemic violence. While the mental health and emotional impacts of victimization are undeniably important, psychological victimology should be complemented by an understanding of how societal structures and situational factors shape the experiences of crime and victimization. In this way, a more holistic approach can be developed to address both the psychological recovery of victims and the broader issues that contribute to their victimization.

Each school of thought in victimology brings unique insights and approaches to understanding victimization, and they often complement one another. By combining perspectives, researchers and policymakers can better address the complex nature of victimization, improving prevention strategies and support systems for victims.

Can compare and contrast all of the discussed schools of thought on victimology, in the Table 1.3.

1.3 Victimology in Relation to Cybercrime

Victimology in the context of cybercrime explores how individuals, organizations, and communities are affected by crimes committed using digital technologies. As cybercrime has become more prevalent with the rise of the internet and digital devices, understanding the experiences of victims within this domain is crucial. Cybercrime victimology focuses on the unique ways in which technology enables crimes such as identity theft, online harassment, cyberbullying, phishing, fraud, and data breaches, among others. This field examines the factors that make certain individuals or organizations more vulnerable to cybercrime and looks at the emotional, financial, and social impacts of these crimes on victims.

Victimology in relation to cybercrime also investigates the role of technology in the victimization process. It considers how technological advancements create new opportunities for criminal behavior, alter the nature of victimization, and affect the reporting and responding to these crimes. For example, cybercrimes often leave victims uncertain about where to report the crime or who is responsible, due to the anonymity and global reach of cyber offenders. Moreover, the emotional impact of cybercrimes, such as the stress from identity theft or the harassment that occurs online, is an area of growing concern, especially when traditional victim support systems may not be equipped to handle the unique aspects of digital victimization.

Table 1.3 Theoretical frameworks of victimology

School of thought	Focus	Characteristics	Criticism
Traditional Victimology	Traditional victimology examines individual and situational factors contributing to victimization, focusing on the victim's characteristics, behaviors, and circumstances	This approach emphasizes risk factors like lifestyle and demographics, using empirical data to identify patterns and inform crime prevention	Traditional victimology risks victim-blaming and overlooking broader social and structural causes of victimization
Critical Victimology	Critical victimology explores how social structures, power dynamics, and inequality shape patterns of victimization, particularly for marginalized groups	This approach is rooted in critical theory, it critiques systemic failures and advocates for addressing root causes like poverty and discrimination	Critical victimology overemphasizes structural factors, potentially neglecting individual agency and situational dynamics
Positivist Victimology	Positivist victimology seeks to identify specific factors that increase the risk of victimization, such as personality traits, lifestyle choices, or social environments. It often uses scientific methods to analyze victimization patterns and aims to make victimization more predictable and preventable	This approach typically involves quantitative data analysis to establish correlations between victim characteristics (like age, gender, or behavior) and crime. It has contributed significantly to victim typologies and risk factors	Positivist victimology has been criticized for potentially leading to victim-blaming, as it sometimes emphasizes how victims' behaviors or characteristics may contribute to their victimization
Feminist Victimology	Feminist victimology centers on how gender and power dynamics contribute to victimization, particularly for women. It highlights issues such as domestic violence, sexual assault, and intimate partner violence, emphasizing that these forms of victimization are often rooted in societal gender inequalities	This approach advocates for policies and support systems that protect and empower victims of gender-based violence. It also promotes research that challenges stereotypes and addresses structural gender-based violence	Some critics argue that it may focus predominantly on female victims and sometimes overlook male victims or other forms of violence not related to gender

(continued)

Table 1.3 (continued)

School of thought	Focus	Characteristics	Criticism
Radical Victimology	Radical victimology examines the role of economic and political structures in creating victimization, particularly focusing on class struggles, inequality, and capitalist systems. It sees victimization as a product of socioeconomic disparities and considers how powerful institutions may exploit or ignore the plight of vulnerable groups	This school of thought builds on Marxist theory, arguing that capitalist systems inherently produce both victims and offenders. It views crime and victimization as expressions of deeper social conflicts and inequalities	Radical victimology's focus on class conflict and economic systems may overlook other forms of identity-based victimization (such as those based on race or gender) and can be seen as overly focused on economic determinism
Victim Precipitation Theory	Victim precipitation theory investigates how victims may inadvertently contribute to their own victimization, either by their behaviors, interactions with offenders, or situational factors. It looks at whether victims play an active or passive role in their victimization	This theory often looks at cases like violent crimes where there may have been a conflict or provocation, attempting to identify patterns where victims' actions contributed to the events	Victim precipitation theory is often criticized for promoting victim-blaming attitudes and for failing to address deeper social and structural causes of crime and victimization
Routine Activity Theory	Routine activity theory (RAT) suggests that victimization occurs when three elements converge: a motivated offender, a suitable target, and a lack of capable guardianship. It looks at the everyday activities and routines of individuals and how these increase or decrease their likelihood of becoming victims	This theory is highly influential in crime prevention, leading to situational crime prevention strategies like increased surveillance or environmental design improvements (e.g., better lighting in public areas)	While practical for crime prevention, RAT is sometimes criticized for its narrow focus on situational factors and lack of consideration for the social context, such as why certain groups may lack "guardianship."

(continued)

Table 1.3 (continued)

School of thought	Focus	Characteristics	Criticism
Lifestyle-Exposure Theory	Lifestyle-exposure theory examines how certain lifestyles or behaviors can increase an individual's risk of victimization. It suggests that people who engage in certain activities (e.g., frequenting high-crime areas or staying out late) may be at higher risk	This theory emphasizes that victimization risk is not random but often correlates with lifestyle choices, and it has informed some crime prevention strategies aimed at personal risk management	Critics argue that this theory can inadvertently encourage victim-blaming by focusing on the choices of victims rather than addressing broader social structures
Developmental Victimology	Developmental victimology examines how victimization impacts individuals across different stages of their lives, particularly childhood and adolescence. It emphasizes the lasting effects of early victimization on later life outcomes	This approach often looks at psychological impacts, such as trauma, and seeks to understand how victimization experiences shape development. It has been influential in fields like child protection and in designing trauma-informed care	Developmental victimology can be limited by its focus on individual psychological factors without fully addressing societal and systemic causes of victimization

(continued)

Table 1.3 (continued)

School of thought	Focus	Characteristics	Criticism
Ecological Victimology	Ecological victimology views victimization within a broader environmental and social context, considering how neighborhoods, communities, and social networks impact victimization risk	This approach looks at how social and physical environments influence crime, such as neighborhood crime rates, community cohesion, and collective efficacy. It's useful for understanding the role of place and social networks in victimization	Ecological victimology can be limited by its geographic focus, sometimes overlooking individual-level factors and broader systemic issues
Psychological Victimology	Psychological victimology looks at the mental and emotional effects of victimization on individuals, studying how trauma, stress, and coping mechanisms develop in victims. It often examines victimization through psychological frameworks like PTSD	This approach has led to insights into trauma-informed care, victim recovery, and mental health interventions for victims	Psychological victimology's individual-level focus may sometimes overlook the structural and situational factors that contribute to victimization in the first place

Cybercrime victimology also examines how the justice system and other societal institutions respond to digital victimization. It looks at issues such as legal frameworks, law enforcement responses, privacy protections, and victim support services in the digital age. As digital crimes evolve, victimology plays an important role in informing policies and practices that can better support victims and prevent future cybercrimes. The goal is to understand not only the experiences and needs of victims in the cybercrime context but also how broader social structures, technological environments, and laws can work together to mitigate the risks and consequences of such victimization.

1.3.1 Cybercrime

Cybercrime refers to criminal activities that involve the use of computers, networks, or digital devices as either the target or the means of committing illegal acts. These crimes are often carried out through the internet or other digital platforms, and they can have a wide range of impacts on individuals, organizations, and governments. Cybercrimes can be categorized based on their nature, targets, and the techniques used. Here are the main categories:

1. **Crimes Against Individuals**

These crimes directly target individuals, often aiming to steal personal information, harm reputations, or exploit victims financially. Examples include:

- Identity Theft
- Phishing and Spear Phishing
- Cyberbullying and Harassment
- Online Stalking
- Fraudulent Emails or Scams

2. **Crimes Against Property**

These involve theft, damage, or illegal access to digital assets and property. Examples include:

- Hacking and Unauthorized Access
- Ransomware Attacks
- Intellectual Property Theft
- Credit Card Fraud
- Data Breaches

3. **Crimes Against Organizations**

Targeting businesses, government agencies, or non-profits to disrupt operations, steal sensitive data, or harm reputations. Examples include:

- Corporate Espionage

- Distributed Denial of Service (DDoS) Attacks
- Insider Threats
- Supply Chain Attacks
- Website Defacement

4. **Crimes Against Governments (Cyberterrorism)**

Crimes targeting national security or infrastructure, often politically motivated. Examples include:

- Espionage (e.g., stealing state secrets)
- Cyberterrorism (e.g., disrupting critical infrastructure)
- Election Interference
- Propaganda and Misinformation Campaigns

5. **Financial Cybercrimes**

Crimes with financial motives, targeting individuals, organizations, or financial institutions. Examples include:

- Online Fraud and Scams
- Money Laundering
- Cryptocurrency Theft
- Bank Fraud and ATM Hacking

6. **Content-Related Cybercrimes**

Involves illegal content distribution or activities using online platforms. Examples include:

- Child Exploitation and Abuse Material
- Illegal Content Hosting (e.g., pirated software, media)
- Hate Speech and Extremism Promotion
- Cyberpornography

7. **Crimes Related to Malware and Exploits**

Focus on disrupting, damaging, or compromising systems using malicious software. Examples include:

- Virus and Worm Attacks
- Spyware and Adware Deployment
- Keylogging and Credential Harvesting
- Botnet Operations

8. **Emerging Cybercrimes**

New types of crimes arising from advancements in technology. Examples include:

- Deepfake Manipulation
- AI-Driven Fraud

- IoT-Based Attacks
- Smart City Infrastructure Hacks

Cybercrime poses significant threats to personal privacy, business security, and national security. The rise of digital technologies and the increasing reliance on the internet for daily activities have made individuals and organizations more vulnerable to cybercriminal activity. The consequences of cybercrime can be severe, ranging from financial loss and reputational damage to emotional trauma and breaches of privacy. As a result, addressing cybercrime involves a combination of legal measures, cybersecurity protocols, and public awareness efforts.

1.3.2 Victimology in Cybercrime vs. Other Types of Crime

Victimology in cybercrime differs from traditional victimology in several key ways due to the unique nature of digital technologies and the virtual environment in which cybercrimes occur. While both fields seek to understand the experiences of victims, the factors that contribute to victimization, and the consequences for the victims, the characteristics of cybercrime create distinct challenges and dynamics in the victimization process. Here are some important ways in which victimology in cybercrime differs:

1. **Anonymity of Offenders**:

One of the most significant differences between cybercrime victimology and traditional victimology is the anonymity of offenders. Cybercriminals often operate under the guise of anonymity provided by the internet, making it difficult for victims to identify or track the perpetrator. This anonymity can increase the psychological distress for victims, as they may not know who is responsible for the crime or whether the offender is still targeting them. In contrast, traditional crimes typically involve more identifiable offenders, allowing for a clearer understanding of the victim-offender relationship.

2. **Global Nature and Jurisdictional Issues**:

Cybercrime often transcends national borders, meaning that offenders can be located anywhere in the world, while the victims might be in a different jurisdiction. This global nature creates complexities in law enforcement and victim support, as different countries may have varying laws, technological infrastructures, and resources to address cybercrime. In traditional crimes, law enforcement and victimology tend to focus on more localized and defined legal frameworks within a specific jurisdiction.

3. **Type of Victimization**:

Traditional victimology primarily focuses on physical crimes, such as theft, assault, or robbery, where victims experience direct physical harm or trauma. In cybercrime victimology, however, the victimization often involves intangible or digital harm, such as identity theft, data breaches, financial fraud, and online harassment. While traditional crimes may cause physical injury or property loss, the emotional, financial, and reputational damages in cybercrime may be less visible but still profound. Victims may also experience stress, confusion, or a lack of support due to the virtual nature of the crime.

4. **Digital vs. Physical Evidence**:

In cybercrime victimology, the evidence is typically digital (e.g., emails, IP addresses, logs, or data) rather than physical (e.g., fingerprints or physical objects). This creates a different set of challenges for victimologists, as digital evidence may be difficult to collect, preserve, or interpret, and it may be easily altered or destroyed. In traditional crimes, physical evidence plays a more central role in identifying offenders and supporting victim claims, making it more straightforward for victims to seek justice.

5. **Victim Reporting and Awareness**:

Many cybercrimes go unreported because victims may not be aware they have been victimized until much later or may not know how or where to report the crime. Victims of online fraud or identity theft may not realize their information has been stolen until they see the consequences months later, and they might feel powerless or unsure about reporting the crime due to its digital nature. In contrast, victims of traditional crimes are often aware of the victimization immediately (e.g., a robbery or physical assault), and there are well-established systems for reporting such crimes.

6. **Long-term Consequences and Recovery**:

The impacts of cybercrime on victims can be more prolonged and subtle, particularly with cases like identity theft, online harassment, or cyberbullying. Victims may experience ongoing emotional distress, reputational damage, or financial consequences, which may persist long after the crime has occurred. The psychological recovery from cybercrime victimization can be complicated by the persistent nature of digital footprints, online harassment, or continuous exposure to malicious content. In contrast, traditional crime victims may have more tangible support systems, and their recovery processes, while still difficult, may be more immediate and recognized by society.

7. **Victim Blaming and Stigma**:

In the case of cybercrime, victims may face a higher degree of victim-blaming, especially in cases like online scams, phishing, or data breaches. Victims may be perceived as lacking the necessary precautions or knowledge to protect themselves, even though the technology is often designed to be complex and rapidly evolving. In traditional crimes, victim-blaming also occurs (e.g., in cases of sexual assault or domestic violence), but the dynamics may differ, and there may be more societal recognition of the victim's experience of harm.

In summary, while victimology in both cybercrime and traditional crime seeks to understand victim experiences, the key differences arise from the virtual nature of cybercrime, the anonymity of offenders, global jurisdictional issues, and the unique challenges of reporting, evidence collection, and long-term recovery for cybercrime victims. The increasing prevalence of cybercrime requires victimology to evolve and adapt to the digital environment, with new frameworks and interventions focused on the specific needs of cybercrime victims.

1.3.3 Cybervictimization

Cyber victimization refers to the experience of becoming a victim of a crime or harmful act that occurs through the use of digital technology, primarily the internet, and computer networks. It involves the victim being targeted by cybercriminals, who exploit technology to inflict harm, whether through financial, emotional, psychological, or reputational damage. Cyber victimization can encompass a wide range of online crimes, such as identity theft, online fraud, cyberbullying, harassment, data breaches, phishing attacks, and more.

Key characteristics of cyber victimization include:

1. **Anonymity and Distance**: Cybercriminals often remain anonymous or untraceable, which can increase the psychological harm for victims, as they may not know who is targeting them. The geographic distance between the victim and the offender also complicates identification and response.
2. **Emotional and Psychological Impact**: The effects of cyber victimization can be long-lasting, leading to stress, anxiety, depression, or a sense of vulnerability. Victims of online harassment or cyberbullying, for instance, may experience significant emotional distress, and the anonymous nature of the crime can make it more difficult to resolve.
3. **Financial Loss**: Cybercrime can also result in substantial financial harm. Common forms of financial cyber victimization include phishing attacks, online scams, and identity theft, where victims may lose money or have their financial information misused for fraudulent activities.
4. **Data and Privacy Breaches**: In cases of data breaches or hacking, victims may experience the theft of personal, private, or sensitive information, which can be exploited for malicious purposes, including financial fraud or blackmail.
5. **Difficulty Reporting and Recovery**: One challenge with cyber victimization is that it can be harder for victims to report the crime or seek assistance due to lack of awareness, uncertainty about where to report, or the global nature of cybercrime that may involve offenders across multiple jurisdictions.

In essence, cyber victimization reflects the growing intersection of technology and crime, with victims facing new and evolving threats that can be difficult to address using traditional methods of crime prevention and response.

1.4 Chapter Summary

Victimology, the study of crime victims, offers valuable insights into the complex nature of victimization and the varied experiences of those affected by crime. From traditional forms of victimization to more modern challenges such as cybercrime, the field has evolved to address the diverse dynamics of victim-offender relationships and the broader societal, psychological, and situational factors influencing these experiences.

The chapter explored various schools of thought in victimology, each contributing distinct perspectives to understanding victimization. Traditional victimology provides foundational insights into the social, psychological, and environmental factors that shape victim experiences. Critical victimology challenges these views by emphasizing power dynamics and structural inequalities in society. Meanwhile, schools like radical victimology, victim precipitation theory, and routine activity theory focus on systemic structures, victim behavior, and environmental conditions that increase vulnerability to victimization. Lifestyle-exposure theory, developmental victimology, ecological victimology, and psychological victimology further broaden the understanding of how individual choices, social environments, and mental health factors intersect to influence victimization. Despite criticisms, these schools offer valuable frameworks for addressing and preventing victimization from multiple angles.

The emergence of cybercrime introduces new dimensions of victimology, requiring adaptation to digital spaces and the complexities of the internet. Victimology in cybercrime considers the anonymity of offenders, the global reach of cybercrimes, and the challenges in reporting and recovering from digital victimization. Unlike traditional crimes, the consequences of cybercrime often involve intangible harm, such as financial loss, reputational damage, and emotional distress, which may be difficult to address with existing support systems. The rise of cybercrime underscores the importance of integrating victimology with technological advancements, highlighting the need for new frameworks and policies that consider the evolving nature of crime and victimization.

Ultimately, a comprehensive understanding of victimology requires a synthesis of the insights from traditional and emerging theories. As society continues to confront both conventional and novel forms of crime, the field of victimology must adapt, focusing not only on the immediate impacts of victimization but also on the broader systemic and technological factors that shape the experiences of victims. By combining theoretical perspectives with practical applications, victimology can better inform prevention strategies, support services, and policies that reduce harm and promote justice for all victims, both offline and online.

Chapter 2
Cybercrime and Cybervictimization

2.1 General Categories of Crime

Crime can be categorized in a handful of different ways, depending on the purpose of the categorization. Generally speaking, crimes can be broken down based on the type of victim, the type of perpetrator, the method of the crime, and the impact of the crime.

Victimologists analyze a variety of crime categories to understand the nature of victimization and its effects on individuals and society, many of which are beyond just cybercrime. These categories often help to focus on the specific dynamics of victimization, such as the relationship between the victim and the offender, the type of harm caused, and the societal factors involved. We will start by exploring the various types of crimes analyzed by victimologists before we proceed to discussing the subsets of cybercriminal activity.

Each of these crime categories allows victimologists to focus on the different patterns, causes, and consequences of victimization, offering insights into prevention strategies, victim support, and broader social interventions.

2.1.1 Personal Crimes

Personal crimes involve offenses where the victim directly suffers physical harm or the threat of harm. These crimes typically target the individual's bodily integrity, sense of safety, and personal well-being.

M. K. A. Lukings et al., *Understanding Cybercrime Victim Services*, Progress in IS,
https://doi.org/10.1007/978-3-032-13273-4_2

2.1.1.1 Violent Crimes

Violent crimes are the most common type of personal crime, and they include offenses such as assault, homicide, sexual assault, robbery, and domestic violence. Assault can range from a physical altercation between individuals to more severe acts such as aggravated assault, where the perpetrator causes serious injury to the victim. Homicide refers to the unlawful killing of a person, which can vary from murder to manslaughter depending on the intent and circumstances surrounding the crime. Robbery involves the use of force, threat, or intimidation to steal from the victim, often leaving emotional and psychological trauma, in addition to the financial loss. Domestic violence, a particularly insidious form of violent crime, occurs within the confines of a home or intimate relationship, where one partner or family member uses physical or emotional violence to control or harm the other.

2.1.1.2 Sexual Crimes

Sexual crimes represent another critical category of personal crimes. These offenses involve non-consensual sexual acts or behaviors that violate the personal autonomy and dignity of the victim. This category includes crimes such as rape, sexual assault, and sexual harassment. Rape refers to the forced or coerced act of sexual intercourse without the victim's consent, often causing severe physical and emotional trauma. Sexual assault may include a range of unwanted sexual activities, from groping to more severe violations. The psychological effects on victims can be profound, including post-traumatic stress disorder (PTSD), anxiety, depression, and feelings of shame or guilt. Sexual harassment, though less violent than assault, still constitutes a violation of personal space and boundaries. It typically involves repeated unwanted sexual advances, comments, or behaviors that create a hostile environment for the victim.

Victimologists study these crimes not only to understand the immediate harm to victims but also to examine the broader societal and cultural factors that enable such crimes, including gender norms, power dynamics, and victim-blaming. The emotional and psychological toll of these offenses can be long-lasting, often affecting victims' relationships, self-esteem, and overall mental health.

2.1.2 Property Crimes

Property crimes are offenses where the primary harm involves the theft or damage of material possessions. These crimes do not typically result in physical harm to the victim but can cause significant emotional distress, financial loss, and a sense of vulnerability.

2.1.2.1 Burglary and Theft

Burglary and theft are among the most common property crimes, where individuals or organizations are targeted for their possessions. Burglary involves breaking into a building, typically a home or business, with the intent to steal property or commit another crime, such as vandalism. Victimologists study the emotional toll that burglary can take on victims, as it often violates their sense of safety and security within their own spaces. Larceny, or theft, involves the unlawful taking of someone's property without breaking into a structure or using force. This can include stealing personal belongings, such as wallets, electronics, or jewelry. Auto theft is another prevalent property crime, where vehicles are stolen for resale, parts, or personal use. Victimologists examine not only the financial loss but also the emotional distress caused by the violation of personal property, the inconvenience of losing a vehicle, and the potential for subsequent victimization if the stolen car is used for other criminal activities. Shoplifting is a form of theft that occurs in retail environments, where individuals take merchandise without paying for it. Although shoplifting may seem like a minor crime, its cumulative impact on businesses, including financial losses and the emotional toll on employees who may feel responsible, is often significant.

2.1.2.2 Vandalism

Vandalism is another category of property crime that involves the willful destruction or defacement of property. This can include a variety of acts, such as graffiti, where individuals use spray paint or other materials to deface public or private property. Vandalism also encompasses acts like breaking windows, slashing tires, or damaging public infrastructure, like street signs or benches. While the financial cost of repairs or replacements can be considerable, the emotional impact of vandalism often goes beyond the material loss. Victims of vandalism may feel disrespected or violated, especially when the property damaged holds sentimental or personal value.

Public spaces, such as parks, schools, or government buildings, can also become targets for vandalism, which can lead to a broader sense of insecurity and a loss of community pride. Vandalism can disrupt the daily lives of individuals or entire communities, creating an environment of fear or unease, and prompting a need for greater community involvement or law enforcement attention to prevent further acts of damage.

2.1.3 White-Collar Crimes

White-collar crimes are non-violent offenses typically committed by individuals or organizations in professional or business settings for financial gain. These crimes often involve deceit, fraud, or violation of trust rather than physical force or violence. The term "white-collar crime" reflects the professional or office-based environment in which these crimes are usually committed, contrasting them with more traditional street crimes.

2.1.3.1 Fraud and Scams

Fraud and scams are a broad category of white-collar crimes that primarily involve deceit or misrepresentation for financial gain. These crimes often occur in environments where trust is central, such as financial institutions, online platforms, and businesses. One of the most prevalent forms of fraud is identity theft, where criminals steal personal information, such as credit card details, Social Security numbers, or banking passwords, to commit fraud or make unauthorized purchases. Victimologists study not only the financial impact of identity theft, which can be significant, but also the psychological toll it takes on victims. The fear of having one's identity stolen and the stress of rectifying fraudulent activity can leave long-lasting emotional scars.

Other forms of financial fraud include Ponzi schemes, insider trading, and embezzlement, all of which often involve high-level offenders with access to corporate or institutional funds. For example, in an insurance fraud case, individuals or businesses might intentionally fabricate or exaggerate claims to receive payouts they are not entitled to. Victimologists focus on how these scams erode trust and financial security, often leaving victims with little recourse to recover their losses.

Online scams, such as phishing, fake e-commerce websites, and investment fraud, are increasingly common in the digital age. Victims of online scams may suffer financial losses, reputational damage, and emotional distress, particularly when they fall victim to highly convincing fraudulent schemes that exploit their trust.

2.1.3.2 Corporate Crimes

Corporate crime refers to criminal activities committed by businesses or corporations, typically for financial gain or to protect the company's interests. This category of crime can have widespread effects on employees, consumers, and society. One of the most significant examples of corporate crime involves environmental violations, such as the illegal dumping of hazardous waste or failure to comply with environmental regulations. These violations can lead to long-term damage to ecosystems, public health risks, and severe penalties for the corporations involved. Victimologists examine the broader societal consequences of such actions, focusing on how affected communities suffer from polluted air, water, and soil, which can lead to chronic health issues and a diminished quality of life.

Another form of corporate crime includes unsafe work conditions, where businesses fail to adhere to health and safety regulations, putting employees at risk of injury or death. For instance, factory workers may be exposed to hazardous chemicals or dangerous machinery due to lax safety standards. Victimologists study the psychological and physical harm caused by these unsafe working environments, noting that employees often experience anxiety, stress, or trauma as a result of workplace accidents. Unethical business practices, such as price-fixing, deceptive advertising, or unfair labor practices, are also forms of corporate crime. Victims in these cases might include consumers who are misled or overcharged, employees who face exploitation or poor working conditions, and the broader economy, which may suffer from the negative effects of unfair business conduct. Corporate crimes can cause significant financial damage, undermine consumer confidence, and result in lasting harm to individuals and communities. Victimologists focus on the power dynamics involved, often examining how corporate structures may prioritize profit over the well-being of stakeholders.

2.1.4 Cybercrime

Cybercrime encompasses a broad range of illegal activities that exploit digital platforms, with significant consequences for individuals, businesses, and society as a whole. Among the many forms of cybercrime, several stand out due to their prevalence and impact. These include identity theft, online harassment and cyberbullying, hacking and data breaches, and phishing with social engineering.

2.1.4.1 Identity Theft

Identity theft is a significant cybercrime in which personal information is stolen and used without authorization, often for fraudulent purposes. Cybercriminals gain access to sensitive data such as Social Security numbers, credit card information, or bank account credentials, typically through tactics like hacking, phishing, or malware. Victims of identity theft often face severe financial consequences, such as unauthorized transactions, loans taken out in their name, or drained accounts. The psychological impact can be equally devastating, as victims experience feelings of violation, anxiety, and helplessness. For instance, a victim may discover their credit ruined after a cybercriminal opens fraudulent accounts, requiring significant time and effort to restore financial stability. Victimologists study these crimes to understand their long-term effects on individuals, emphasizing the need for education about data protection and stricter cybersecurity measures.

2.1.4.2 Online Harassment and Cyberbullying

Online harassment and cyberbullying encompass various forms of abusive behavior conducted through digital platforms, such as social media, messaging apps, or emails. These crimes often target individuals based on their identity, opinions, or personal circumstances, making them particularly distressing. Victims of online harassment may receive threatening messages, have their private information (like addresses or photos) shared publicly without consent (a practice known as "doxxing"), or experience sustained campaigns of intimidation. Cyberbullying, which often affects younger individuals, involves repeated acts of humiliation or aggression online, such as spreading rumors, sharing embarrassing images, or creating fake accounts to impersonate and defame the victim. The psychological effects of such crimes can be profound, leading to depression, anxiety, social withdrawal, or even suicidal thoughts. Victimologists explore the societal factors that contribute to such behavior and advocate for stronger legal and technological protections for victims, as well as support systems to aid their recovery.

2.1.4.3 Hacking and Data Breaches

Hacking and data breaches both involve the unauthorized access to computer systems, networks, or data, often with malicious intent. Hackers may target individuals, businesses, or government entities to steal sensitive information, disrupt operations, or gain financial advantage. For example, a data breach at a corporation can expose customers' personal and financial information, leading to widespread identity theft and financial losses. Victimologists examine how such incidents affect not only individual victims but also businesses and society at large. They explore the emotional toll on individuals who fear the misuse of their private data, as well as the economic impact on organizations that face reputational damage and legal consequences. High-profile cases, like breaches of healthcare or financial institutions, highlight the need for robust cybersecurity measures and victim support frameworks.

2.1.4.4 Phishing and Social Engineering

Phishing and social engineering are deceptive tactics used by cybercriminals to manipulate individuals into divulging sensitive information, such as passwords, account details, or credit card numbers. Phishing attacks often take the form of fraudulent emails or messages that mimic legitimate organizations, such as banks or government agencies, urging victims to click on malicious links or provide personal information. For instance, a victim might receive an email claiming to be from their bank, requesting they "verify" their account details, only to have their credentials stolen. Social engineering extends beyond phishing, using psychological manipulation to exploit trust and human error. Examples include phone calls from scammers pretending to be tech support to gain remote access to a victim's computer. Victimologists analyze the methods used in these crimes and their impacts, noting how victims often feel embarrassed or blame themselves for falling prey to such schemes. Education on recognizing and avoiding phishing attempts, combined with technological safeguards, is a crucial focus for mitigating this type of cybercrime.

2.1.5 "Victimless" Crimes

Victimless crimes are often defined as illegal activities that do not have a direct or identifiable victim in the traditional sense, as they usually involve consensual participation among adults. However, victimologists analyze these crimes to uncover hidden or indirect victims, examining how societal structures, exploitation, and associated harms impact individuals and communities.

2.1.5.1 Drug Use and Prostitution

Drug use is often considered a victimless crime because it typically involves a consenting individual choosing to consume illegal substances. However, victimologists explore the broader consequences of drug use, such as addiction, exploitation by drug traffickers, or harm to family members. For example, an individual's drug addiction might lead to financial instability, neglect of dependents, or involvement in criminal activities to sustain their habit, indirectly victimizing others. Additionally, the production and distribution of drugs can have severe societal impacts, such as violence in communities controlled by drug cartels.

Similarly, **prostitution** is frequently described as a victimless crime, especially when it involves consensual adults. However, victimologists delve into the underlying issues of exploitation, coercion, and abuse that often accompany the sex trade. Many individuals, particularly women and children, are forced into prostitution through human trafficking, making them victims of exploitation and violence. Even in cases where individuals willingly engage in prostitution, they may face societal stigmatization, legal consequences, or health risks such as sexually transmitted infections, which can significantly affect their lives. For example, victimologists might study how societal attitudes toward prostitution perpetuate cycles of marginalization and hinder access to healthcare or legal protection.

2.1.5.2 Gambling

Gambling is another activity often regarded as a victimless crime because it typically involves voluntary participation. However, victimologists analyze the darker aspects of gambling, such as problem gambling and its effects on individuals and families. Problem gambling, where individuals are unable to control their gambling habits, can lead to significant financial harm, such as bankruptcy or loss of savings. This, in turn, can impact family members, who may suffer from financial insecurity or emotional distress. For example, a compulsive gambler may drain joint bank accounts, leaving their partner and children financially vulnerable.

Furthermore, gambling can contribute to broader societal issues. The prevalence of gambling addiction in communities can lead to increased demand for social services, healthcare resources, and legal interventions. Victimologists also examine how gambling establishments may exploit vulnerable populations, targeting individuals with low incomes or pre-existing addictions through advertising or predatory practices.

While drug use, prostitution, and gambling may not have a clear victim in every instance, victimologists explore the nuanced and often hidden ways these activities create harm. By understanding the broader social, economic, and psychological impacts, victimologists contribute to the development of policies and interventions aimed at minimizing harm and supporting affected individuals and communities.

2.1.6 Child Abuse and Exploitation

Child abuse and exploitation represent some of the most serious and devastating crimes, leaving lasting impacts on victims and society. Victimologists dedicate significant attention to understanding the causes, consequences, and prevention of these crimes, as well as advocating for the rights and recovery of affected children.

2.1.6.1 Physical and Emotional Abuse

Physical and emotional abuse of children involves actions or neglect by caregivers or others in positions of trust that result in harm or significant risk of harm to a child's physical or emotional well-being. Physical abuse includes acts like hitting, shaking, or burning, which can lead to injuries, developmental issues, or even fatalities. Emotional abuse, on the other hand, includes verbal assaults, threats, rejection, or constant criticism that undermine a child's self-esteem and mental health. For example, a child subjected to constant berating by a parent may struggle with anxiety, depression, and difficulties forming healthy relationships later in life.

Victimologists explore how such abuse impacts children over time, often finding correlations between early abuse and later challenges such as poor academic performance, substance abuse, and criminal behavior. Additionally, researchers examine societal factors, such as poverty, lack of parental support, or cultural norms, that contribute to the prevalence of abuse. Case studies often highlight the profound emotional and psychological scars left by abusive environments, emphasizing the need for intervention and support systems like counseling and child protective services.

2.1.6.2 Sexual Exploitation

Sexual exploitation of children is among the most heinous crimes victimologists study. This includes trafficking children for sexual purposes, producing or distributing child pornography, and online grooming by predators. These acts often involve coercion, manipulation, or outright force, leaving victims physically harmed and emotionally devastated. For instance, children trafficked for sex may be subjected to repeated abuse, deprived of basic needs, and isolated from any form of support or safety.

2.1.6.3 Online Exploitation

Online exploitation is another alarming area, as the internet enables predators to target vulnerable children with relative anonymity. Offenders may coerce children into sharing explicit images or videos, which are then distributed across digital platforms, compounding the harm. Victimologists investigate the long-term effects on victims, such as post-traumatic stress disorder (PTSD), trust issues, and difficulty reintegrating into normal life. For example, a victim whose images are shared online may live in fear of being recognized or judged, even years after the abuse has ended.

Efforts to combat child sexual exploitation often involve multidisciplinary approaches, including law enforcement crackdowns on trafficking networks, international cooperation to remove harmful online content, and victim support services. Victimologists also advocate for stronger legal protections and greater societal awareness to prevent these crimes and support survivors in their recovery.

Overall, child abuse and exploitation are areas where victimology intersects deeply with advocacy, law enforcement, and mental health. By shedding light on the pervasive and long-lasting effects of these crimes, victimologists help to drive efforts aimed at prevention, justice, and healing for the most vulnerable members of society.

2.1.7 Hate Crimes

Hate crimes are offenses driven by prejudice or discrimination against individuals or groups based on characteristics such as race, religion, ethnicity, gender, sexual orientation, disability, or other identity markers. These crimes go beyond the immediate physical or emotional harm to the victim, often targeting their identity and sense of belonging. Victimologists play a crucial role in analyzing the personal and societal impact of these offenses, aiming to understand their root causes and promote strategies to address them.

Hate crimes often manifest in acts of violence, vandalism, threats, or harassment. For example, a racially motivated assault may leave physical scars on a victim while also fostering a pervasive sense of fear and insecurity in the broader community of the targeted group. A synagogue vandalized with anti-Semitic graffiti not only harms the immediate congregation but also sends a message of hostility to all individuals of Jewish faith. Victimologists explore these ripple effects, focusing on how such crimes create climates of fear, division, and alienation for entire communities, not just individual victims.

The psychological harm inflicted by hate crimes is profound, often surpassing the impact of other crimes. Victims may suffer from anxiety, depression, post-traumatic stress disorder (PTSD), or a diminished sense of personal safety. For instance, a transgender individual targeted by a hate crime may face ongoing trauma and isolation, fearing further discrimination or violence in their daily life. Victimologists examine these emotional consequences to advocate for comprehensive support systems, such as counseling, community outreach, and legal protection.

In addition to the individual and communal harm, hate crimes pose a broader threat to social cohesion. They often aim to intimidate and marginalize minority groups, eroding trust in institutions like law enforcement or the justice system if adequate protection and accountability are not ensured. For example, if hate crimes against a particular ethnic group are perceived as being ignored or inadequately addressed by authorities, it can exacerbate feelings of disenfranchisement and mistrust within that community.

Victimologists also study the role of systemic factors and societal prejudices in enabling hate crimes. This includes examining how media representation, political rhetoric, or socioeconomic inequalities can fuel discriminatory attitudes and violence. By addressing these root causes, victimologists contribute to the development of policies and programs aimed at fostering inclusivity, tolerance, and resilience against hate.

Hate crimes are uniquely damaging offenses that attack the core of an individual's identity and the unity of communities. Victimologists work to understand the multifaceted impact of these crimes, advocate for victims, and contribute to initiatives that promote equality and reduce prejudice. Through this work, they help create a more informed and compassionate response to the enduring challenge of hate-based violence and discrimination.

2.1.8 Terrorism

Terrorism is a form of violence that is often politically, ideologically, or religiously motivated, with the intent to instill fear, disrupt societal norms, and achieve specific objectives. While terrorism is primarily analyzed through the lens of politics, security, or ideology, victimologists focus on understanding the profound and multifaceted impact it has on its victims, individuals, communities, and even entire nations.

Victims of terrorism frequently endure severe physical and emotional trauma. For example, survivors of the September 11, 2001 attacks in the United States not only suffered devastating physical injuries but also faced long-term psychological effects such as post-traumatic stress disorder (PTSD), depression, and anxiety. Family members of victims grapple with grief and loss, often compounded by the public and high-profile nature of such events. Victimologists analyze these experiences to advocate for effective support systems, including counseling, medical care, and compensation for survivors and bereaved families.

Beyond the direct victims, terrorism has a far-reaching impact on communities. Attacks often target public spaces or symbolic landmarks, such as markets, schools, or government buildings, aiming to create widespread fear and disrupt daily life. For instance, the 2004 Madrid train bombings and the 2019 Christchurch mosque shootings left not only immediate victims but also entire communities reeling from fear, distrust, and insecurity. Victimologists study how these collective traumas affect social cohesion, intergroup relations, and perceptions of safety.

Terrorism also imposes significant societal consequences, as nations often respond with heightened security measures, surveillance, or policy changes. Victimologists examine how these responses may affect survivors, who may feel further alienated or stigmatized, particularly in cases where their communities are wrongly associated with the perpetrators. For example, in the aftermath of terrorist attacks linked to specific ethnic or religious groups, individuals from those communities may face increased discrimination or hate crimes, compounding their victimization.

Victimologists also explore the ripple effects of terrorism on national identity and resilience. For instance, the 2005 London bombings not only sparked public mourning but also led to significant discussions about multiculturalism, immigration, and societal unity. By analyzing these broader impacts, victimologists contribute to initiatives aimed at fostering resilience and solidarity among affected populations, ensuring that the aftermath of terrorism does not further fracture society.

Finally, victimologists advocate for victims' rights in the context of terrorism. They work to ensure that survivors and families receive recognition, justice, and adequate support. For example, organizations such as the Victims of Terrorism Association in Spain provide a voice for those affected, pushing for fair compensation and representation in public discourse.

In summary, terrorism inflicts extensive harm that transcends physical injury or loss of life, affecting individuals, communities, and nations on multiple levels. Victimologists provide essential insights into these impacts, focusing on the needs of victims and advocating for societal responses that promote healing, justice, and resilience in the face of such atrocities.

2.1.9 State-Sponsored Crimes

State-sponsored crimes refer to acts of harm or violence carried out by government authorities or agents, often under the guise of maintaining law and order, national security, or public policy. Victimologists focus on these crimes to highlight the abuse of power by state actors and the significant impacts on victims and broader societal trust. A key area of study within state-sponsored crimes is police brutality and state violence, where law enforcement or military personnel inflict harm on civilians.

2.1.9.1 Police Brutality

Police brutality involves the excessive use of force by law enforcement officers, which can result in physical injuries, emotional trauma, and even death. High-profile cases such as the killing of George Floyd in the United States in 2020 have drawn global attention to the disproportionate use of force against marginalized communities, particularly Black and Indigenous populations. Victimologists analyze such cases to understand patterns of systemic bias, institutional failures, and the long-term psychological effects on individuals and communities. Victims of police brutality often experience PTSD, depression, and a deep mistrust of law enforcement, which can hinder their willingness to engage with the justice system in the future.

2.1.9.2 State Violence

State violence extends beyond policing and includes actions such as unlawful detentions, torture, and the violent suppression of protests. For instance, during the 2019–2020 protests in Hong Kong, reports of police violence, including the use of tear gas, rubber bullets, and physical assaults against demonstrators, raised significant concerns about human rights violations. Victimologists study the impacts of such actions, not only on direct victims but also on society as a whole, where the erosion of trust in state institutions can lead to long-lasting social and political instability.

One of the critical areas of focus for victimologists is the effect of state-sponsored crimes on marginalized or vulnerable groups. Indigenous communities, for example, have often been subjected to state violence in the context of land disputes, forced assimilation policies, or protest suppression. In Canada, investigations into the treatment of Indigenous women have revealed systemic failures by law enforcement to protect these individuals, sometimes implicating police in acts of violence or neglect. Victimologists examine these patterns to advocate for accountability, justice, and systemic reform.

Another dimension of state-sponsored crimes is the emotional and societal toll on victims. Survivors of police brutality or state violence often face stigma, fear of retaliation, or a sense of powerlessness, knowing that the perpetrators are part of a powerful institution. For example, individuals detained and tortured during military dictatorships, such as those in Argentina's "Dirty War" (1976–1983), frequently suffer from long-term psychological trauma and societal ostracization. Victimologists study these effects to develop support mechanisms and ensure survivors' voices are heard in the pursuit of justice and reconciliation.

State-sponsored crimes represent a significant breach of the trust placed in government institutions to protect citizens. Victimologists play a crucial role in analyzing the individual and collective harm caused by these abuses, highlighting systemic issues, and advocating for reforms to prevent future occurrences. By examining cases of police brutality, unlawful detentions, and state violence, victimologists contribute to the broader goal of ensuring accountability and fostering societal trust in governance and justice systems.

2.1.10 Domestic Violence

Domestic violence is a specific category of violent crime characterized by harm inflicted by intimate partners, family members, or others within a domestic setting. It encompasses various forms of abuse, including physical violence, emotional manipulation, psychological intimidation, financial control, and sexual violence. Victimologists study domestic violence to understand the long-term impacts on victims, the systemic barriers they face, and the broader societal implications of these offenses.

The nature of abuse in domestic violence often involves a pattern of coercive and controlling behavior, where the offender exerts power over the victim. Physical abuse may include acts such as hitting, choking, or other forms of assault that result in injury. For example, in cases where intimate partners engage in sustained physical violence, victims often suffer long-term health consequences, including chronic pain, mobility issues, or traumatic brain injuries. Emotional and psychological abuse, such as constant belittlement, isolation from support networks, or threats of harm, can be equally damaging. Victims may develop anxiety, depression, PTSD, or feelings of helplessness that persist long after the abusive relationship ends.

Barriers to seeking help are a critical area of focus for victimologists. Many victims of domestic violence face significant challenges in leaving abusive situations. Fear of retaliation, financial dependence on the abuser, social stigma, and lack of access to resources or support systems often prevent victims from seeking help. For example, a woman in a financially dependent relationship may hesitate to report abuse or leave her partner due to concerns about supporting herself or her children. Cultural factors can also play a role; in some communities, domestic violence may be dismissed as a private family matter, discouraging victims from speaking out.

The psychological effects of domestic violence are profound and far-reaching. Victims often experience a cycle of hope and despair, with periods of reconciliation and promises of change followed by repeated abuse. Over time, this cycle can erode a victim's self-esteem and sense of agency, making it harder to escape the situation. For instance, survivors of long-term emotional abuse frequently report feeling as though they are to blame for the violence, a perception often reinforced by the abuser. Victimologists work to dismantle these harmful narratives, emphasizing that the responsibility for abuse lies solely with the offender.

The societal impact of domestic violence extends beyond the immediate victim. Children who witness domestic violence in the home often experience developmental delays, emotional disturbances, and difficulty forming healthy relationships later in life. These intergenerational effects underscore the importance of addressing domestic violence not only for individual victims but also for families and communities as a whole.

Victimologists also examine institutional responses to domestic violence, such as the role of law enforcement, social services, and healthcare providers. Effective interventions, such as restraining orders, shelters for victims, counseling services, and public awareness campaigns, are critical in supporting survivors and preventing future abuse. However, systemic shortcomings, such as insufficient training for law enforcement or inadequate funding for support services, often leave victims vulnerable.

One notable example is the case of domestic violence shelters, which provide a safe space for victims but may have limited capacity or funding. In rural areas, victims may face additional barriers due to geographical isolation or lack of nearby resources. Victimologists highlight these disparities to advocate for more comprehensive and accessible support systems.

Domestic violence is a pervasive issue that inflicts significant harm on individuals, families, and communities. Victimologists play a crucial role in uncovering the complexities of domestic violence, studying its psychological effects, identifying systemic barriers to assistance, and advocating for policies and programs that empower victims to escape abuse and rebuild their lives. By addressing the root causes and consequences of domestic violence, victimology contributes to creating safer and more supportive environments for survivors.

2.2 Understanding Cybercrime

In today's world, where digital devices and the internet have become essential parts of our lives, cybercrime has emerged as a significant and growing threat. Cybercrime refers to illegal activities that are carried out using computers, digital devices, or the internet. These activities can range from stealing personal information to hacking systems or spreading malicious software (malware). As technology continues to evolve, so do the methods used by cybercriminals, making it crucial for individuals, businesses, and governments to understand the various types of cybercrimes and how to protect themselves.

Cybercrime encompasses illegal actions that exploit vulnerabilities in technology or the internet. These activities are typically carried out with the intent of causing harm, stealing data, or gaining financial benefits. The increase in cybercrime in recent years is partly due to the widespread use of the internet and digital technologies. These technologies, which connect billions of people worldwide, have also become tools for criminals seeking to exploit individuals, organizations, and even governments.

While cybercriminals are often motivated by financial gain, they can also commit crimes for political or personal reasons. Some cybercriminals operate solo, while others are part of highly organized groups that engage in complex cyberattacks. In some cases, cybercriminals may employ advanced techniques to execute their attacks, while in other cases, less experienced criminals may use simpler tools or methods.

2.2.1 *Types of Cybercrime*

Cybercrime can be classified into several types based on the nature of the offense and the methods used by criminals. These crimes may be categorized as **cyber-enabled crimes**, **cyber-dependent crimes**, **computer-supported crimes**, and even **cyberterrorism**.

Cyber-Enabled Crimes:

These are traditional crimes that have been expanded or facilitated through the use of technology. Examples include fraud, identity theft, and harassment, which leverage digital platforms to reach broader audiences or execute faster.

Cyber-Dependent Crimes:

These crimes cannot exist without the use of technology, as they directly target or exploit digital systems. Examples include hacking, ransomware attacks, or DDoS attacks.

Computer-Supported Crimes:

These are crimes where technology plays a supportive role but is not essential to the crime itself. For example, using a computer to plan or coordinate illegal activities, such as trafficking or money laundering.

Cyberterrorism:

This involves using digital technologies to instill fear, disrupt critical infrastructure, or compromise national security. Examples include attacks on power grids, propaganda dissemination, or espionage.

The four categories, **cyber-enabled crimes**, **cyber-dependent crimes**, **computer-supported crimes**, and **cyberterrorism,** defined by offenses and methodologies align closely with broader cybersecurity categorizations which has been listed in chapter one. For example, Cyber-enabled crimes map to **Crimes Against Individuals** and **Crimes Against Organizations**, as they exploit digital platforms to amplify traditional offenses. Cyber-dependent crimes directly correspond to **Crimes Against Property** and **Emerging Cybercrimes**, as they rely entirely on digital systems. Computer-supported crimes share similarities with **Content-Related Cybercrimes**, where technology aids but does not define the crime. Finally, cyberterrorism is a direct match with **Crimes Against Governments**, focusing on politically or ideologically motivated attacks on national security. Here we will explain the main categories in detail.

2.2.1.1 Hacking

Hacking refers to unauthorized access to computer systems or networks with the intent to steal, alter, or destroy data. Hackers often exploit vulnerabilities in software or hardware to gain control over systems. Once inside, they may steal sensitive information, disrupt operations, or install malicious software to further compromise the system.

For example, a hacker might break into a company's internal network and steal valuable intellectual property, such as customer data, business secrets, or research and development materials. This information can then be used for financial gain, sold on the dark web, or used to damage the organization's reputation.

2.2.1.2 Phishing

Phishing is a deceptive practice where cybercriminals impersonate legitimate organizations or individuals to trick victims into revealing sensitive information, such as usernames, passwords, and credit card details. This is typically done through fraudulent emails, phone calls, or websites designed to look authentic.

An example of phishing might involve a hacker sending an email that appears to come from a victim's bank, asking them to click on a link and verify their account details. The link directs the victim to a fake website where they unknowingly provide their information to the attacker.

2.2.1.3 Ransomware

Ransomware is a type of malware that encrypts files or entire systems, rendering them inaccessible to the victim. The attacker then demands a ransom, usually paid in cryptocurrency, in exchange for a decryption key to restore access to the data. In some cases, the hacker may threaten to release the stolen data publicly if the ransom is not paid.

For example, a healthcare provider might fall victim to a ransomware attack, with patient records being locked away until the organization pays the ransom. The threat of exposing sensitive medical data can put the business under extreme pressure to comply with the attacker's demands.

2.2.1.4 Identity Theft

Identity theft occurs when a cybercriminal steals personal information, such as a person's name, Social Security number, or bank account details, to impersonate them for financial gain. Cybercriminals may use the stolen identity to open credit accounts, make unauthorized purchases, or commit fraud.

For example, an attacker might steal an individual's credit card information and make fraudulent purchases or transfer funds to offshore accounts. In some cases, identity theft can go undetected for months, making recovery of lost assets and restoring one's identity a long and painful process.

2.2.1.5 Online Scams

Online scams involve various fraudulent schemes conducted over the internet. These scams often include fake websites, fake online stores, or deceptive advertisements designed to trick individuals into providing personal information or paying for products and services that don't exist.

An example of an online scam could be a fraudulent e-commerce website that mimics a popular retail brand. Victims may make a purchase, but never receive the product, and the scammer disappears with their money.

2.2.1.6 Malware

Malware is malicious software designed to damage or gain unauthorized access to computer systems. There are various types of malware, including viruses, worms, trojans, and spyware, each with different methods of spreading and attacking.

For instance, a trojan horse may be disguised as a legitimate program or file, but once installed, it opens a backdoor to allow hackers to access the infected system remotely. This could lead to data theft or a broader network compromise.

2.2.1.7 Denial-of-Service (DoS) Attacks

A **Denial-of-Service (DoS)** attack occurs when a hacker overwhelms a network or server with an enormous amount of traffic, effectively preventing legitimate users from accessing the system or services. DoS attacks can disrupt websites, online services, or even entire networks.

For example, a hacker might flood a company's website with traffic to prevent customers from making purchases or accessing information during a critical sales event, leading to financial loss and reputational damage.

2.2.1.8 Cyberbullying

Cyberbullying refers to the use of digital platforms to harass, intimidate, or humiliate an individual. This form of harassment can occur via social media, text messages, or email. The effects of cyberbullying can be devastating, especially for young people, as it can lead to emotional distress, anxiety, or even suicidal thoughts.

A common example of cyberbullying might involve someone spreading harmful rumors or sharing embarrassing photos of another person online without their consent, causing significant personal and professional harm to the victim.

2.2.1.9 Data Breaches

Data breaches occur when unauthorized individuals gain access to sensitive personal or corporate information. The stolen data can then be used for identity theft, financial fraud, or espionage.

For instance, a data breach at a major retailer might expose millions of customers' personal details, such as names, addresses, and credit card numbers. This puts individuals at risk of identity theft and financial loss.

2.2.1.10 Financial Fraud

Financial fraud is any criminal activity that involves deceiving individuals or organizations for monetary gain. Examples of financial fraud include online banking fraud, credit card fraud, and investment scams.

For example, a cybercriminal might send a fraudulent email pretending to be from a bank's security team, asking the recipient to update their banking information. Once the victim complies, the attacker can steal funds directly from their account.

2.2.1.11 Cyber Espionage

Cyber espionage involves the use of digital tools to steal classified or sensitive information from governments, corporations, or individuals. It is often conducted for political, economic, or military advantage.

An example of cyber espionage could be a government-backed hacker group infiltrating a company's network to steal trade secrets or sensitive information that could be used to gain an advantage in negotiations or to undermine national security.

2.2.2 Cybercrime Methodology

Cybercrime operates through various methods and techniques that exploit weaknesses in systems, networks, or human behavior. Cybercriminals use various strategies to typically carry out their attacks, which we will explore here.

- **Reconnaissance:**

  Cybercriminals often perform reconnaissance before identifying vulnerabilities. This involves gathering information about the target, such as open ports, employee details, or network architecture, often using tools like Nmap or social media.

- **Weaponization:**

This stage involves creating or acquiring tools like malware, exploits, or phishing kits that will be used during the attack.

- **Exploitation:**

  Once access is gained, attackers exploit specific vulnerabilities to escalate privileges, move laterally within the system, or target specific assets.

- **Command and Control (C2):**

  In advanced attacks, cybercriminals establish persistent remote access to the compromised system using C2 servers, enabling them to control and execute further operations.

- **Data Exfiltration:**

  After the initial execution, attackers may focus on extracting sensitive data, such as intellectual property, credentials, or customer information, often transferring it to external servers.

- **Persistence:**

  Cybercriminals often install backdoors or maintain access by creating hidden user accounts, ensuring they can return to the system even if the initial attack vector is discovered and closed.

- **Monetization:**

  After completing the attack, criminals often monetize their efforts by selling stolen data on the dark web, demanding ransoms, or using stolen credentials for financial fraud.

- **Post-Exploitation Activities:**

  Advanced attackers may manipulate the data they access, install further malicious software, or use the compromised system as a springboard for attacking other networks.

- **Botnet Building:**

  - Attackers may infect systems to turn them into bots, which can then be used for launching larger attacks, like DDoS or spam campaigns.

- **Supply Chain Attacks:**

  Instead of attacking a primary target directly, cybercriminals compromise third-party vendors or software providers to infiltrate the target's ecosystem.

2.2.3 Legal Remedies for Cybercrime

Governments around the world have recognized the growing threat of cybercrime and have implemented laws to protect individuals, organizations, and nations from online threats. Legal frameworks play a critical role in addressing cybercrime, as they provide the tools needed for law enforcement to prosecute cybercriminals.

Cybercrime Laws

Governments have created specific laws designed to address cybercrime. These laws often target activities like hacking, data theft, fraud, and the spread of malware. For example, the Computer Fraud and Abuse Act (CFAA) in the United States criminalizes unauthorized access to computer systems and data.

Law Enforcement Agencies

To combat cybercrime, specialized law enforcement agencies or cybercrime units have been established to investigate and prosecute cybercriminals. These agencies often work internationally to tackle crimes that span borders.

International Cooperation

Since cybercrime is often committed across borders, international cooperation is essential in fighting it. Countries work together to share information, support investigations, and extradite criminals for prosecution.

Regulatory Compliance

Organizations must comply with cybersecurity regulations to protect data and minimize the risk of breaches. This includes implementing measures to safeguard against cyberattacks, encrypt sensitive data, and respond swiftly to security incidents.

Victim Support Services

If you become a victim of cybercrime, there are support services available that offer legal advice, psychological counseling, and resources for recovering from the crime. These services can help victims navigate the aftermath of cybercrimes such as identity theft or online harassment.

As technology continues to evolve, cybercrime will likely become an even greater threat. Understanding the various types of cybercrime, their impacts, and the legal remedies available is crucial for protecting ourselves and our communities in the digital age. By staying informed, using strong security measures, and collaborating globally, we can reduce the risk of falling victim to cybercriminals and work toward a safer and more secure online environment for all.

2.3 Victim Support Services for Cybercrime Victims

Cybercrime victims often face significant challenges not only in dealing with the immediate consequences of the crime but also in navigating the emotional and psychological impact. Victim support services play a crucial role in helping individuals and organizations recover from cybercrimes and protect themselves from further harm. These services are designed to provide both practical and emotional assistance to those affected by various forms of cybercrime, ranging from identity theft and online fraud to cyberbullying and data breaches.

2.3.1 Legal Assistance

One of the first types of support victims may require is legal assistance. Navigating the legal system after a cybercrime incident can be overwhelming, especially if the victim needs to pursue legal action against the attacker. Victim support services often provide guidance on how to report the crime to law enforcement and offer information on relevant laws and regulations. For example, in the case of identity theft, victims may need to understand their rights under privacy laws or how to freeze their credit with financial institutions. Additionally, some services provide legal professionals who can help victims with issues such as filing complaints, recovering losses, or seeking restitution.

2.3.2 Emotional and Psychological Support

Cybercrime can take a severe toll on a victim's mental health. The anxiety of having personal or financial information stolen, the embarrassment of being targeted by cyberbullying, or the fear of further attacks can lead to stress, depression, and even post-traumatic stress disorder (PTSD).

Psychological counseling and emotional support services are vital in helping victims cope with the aftermath of the crime. Many victim services offer counseling for those experiencing distress, especially in cases involving online harassment or cyberbullying.

Support groups and peer-to-peer networks can also help victims feel less isolated, as they can share their experiences with others who have gone through similar situations. These support systems help empower victims to regain control and rebuild their lives after the incident.

2.3.3 *Identity Recovery and Financial Assistance*

For crimes like identity theft or financial fraud, victim support services may offer specialized recovery programs. These services assist victims in restoring their identities, monitoring their credit, and recovering stolen funds. Many organizations offer identity theft protection services, which include monitoring credit reports, helping to remove fraudulent accounts from the victim's name, and providing access to resources that help rebuild damaged financial reputations.

Victims of financial cybercrimes may also receive assistance in navigating the process of filing claims with banks, credit card companies, or insurance providers. In some cases, government agencies or nonprofit organizations may offer financial compensation or help victims recover funds that were lost during a cybercrime event.

2.3.4 *Technical Assistance*

In cases of data breaches, hacking, or ransomware attacks, technical assistance is often necessary to secure systems, remove malware, and prevent further damage. Victim support services may offer access to cybersecurity experts who can help restore compromised systems, advise on securing personal or business networks, and protect against future attacks. For example, after a ransomware attack, victims may need help decrypting files, recovering from data loss, and securing their devices from additional malware.

In the case of phishing or malware infections, technical support might include guidance on how to remove malicious software, change passwords, or report compromised accounts to relevant platforms, such as social media sites or online banking institutions.

2.3.5 *Reporting and Advocacy*

Victim services also play an important role in helping individuals report cybercrimes to the appropriate authorities. They can assist in contacting law enforcement, filing reports with regulatory bodies, and tracking the progress of investigations. Some organizations, such as the Internet Crime Complaint Center (IC3) in the U.S., offer online platforms for reporting cybercrime. These agencies work with global law enforcement partners to investigate cross-border cybercrime and bring perpetrators to justice.

Additionally, victim support services often advocate for stronger cybercrime laws and better protections for vulnerable individuals. These organizations may lobby for legislation that addresses emerging threats, such as new forms of cyberbullying or online harassment, and work to raise public awareness about the importance of cybersecurity.

2.3.6 Educational Resources and Prevention

Victim support services often provide educational resources to help individuals understand how to protect themselves from future cybercrimes. This can include information on safe internet practices, how to recognize phishing scams, the importance of strong passwords, and how to implement multi-factor authentication. By offering prevention tips and proactive guidance, these services empower victims to strengthen their cybersecurity awareness and reduce the risk of future incidents.

Support services might also help businesses implement cybersecurity measures, such as employee training on recognizing cyber threats or improving internal security policies to safeguard customer data.

2.3.7 Advocacy and Public Awareness Campaigns

In addition to assisting individual victims, support services often engage in **public awareness campaigns** to educate the wider community about the dangers of cybercrime. These campaigns are designed to promote safe online behavior, reduce stigma associated with being a cybercrime victim, and encourage individuals to report incidents of cybercrime. By increasing public awareness, these campaigns can help prevent others from falling victim to similar attacks.

2.3.8 Goals of Victim Services

Victim support services for cybercrime victims are essential in helping individuals and businesses recover from the emotional, financial, and technical consequences of a cyberattack. By offering legal assistance, psychological support, identity recovery services, technical help, and educational resources, these services provide a comprehensive approach to assisting victims in rebuilding their lives and protecting themselves from future attacks. In addition, advocacy and awareness campaigns play a crucial role in the broader fight against cybercrime, helping to ensure that victims are not left to navigate the aftermath alone.

2.4 Challenges Specific to Victims of Cybercrime

Victims of cybercrime face unique challenges that distinguish their experiences from victims of more traditional, non-digital crimes. The nature of cybercrime, its invisibility, global reach, and ever-evolving tactics, creates a distinctive set of problems for victims. Below, we explore several key factors that make cybercrime victims' experiences different from those who suffer from other types of crime.

2.4.1 Perpetrator Anonymity

One of the most significant differences between cybercrime and traditional crime is the anonymity that cybercriminals often enjoy. Unlike physical crimes where perpetrators are more likely to be seen or identified, cybercriminals can operate from virtually anywhere in the world, often hiding behind layers of technology to mask their identities. This makes it harder for victims to comprehend who is responsible for the crime, and the lack of physical evidence can make it more difficult for law enforcement to track down and prosecute offenders.

For example, in a case of identity theft where personal information is stolen through a phishing attack, the victim may never know who accessed their data or how it was used. This anonymity can exacerbate feelings of powerlessness and frustration, as victims feel that they have no control over their situation or recourse for justice.

2.4.2 Psychological and Emotional Impact

While all types of crime can have psychological and emotional consequences for victims, the impact of cybercrime can be especially insidious. In cases of cyberbullying, revenge porn, or online harassment, the harm is often prolonged and persistent. Victims may experience ongoing distress from the constant accessibility of the internet, where harmful content can be shared with a broad audience, potentially reaching millions of people within seconds.

Additionally, victims of cybercrime often feel a sense of invasion that differs from the violation felt in physical crimes. Cybercrimes such as hacking, data breaches, or surveillance can feel deeply personal, as they often involve intimate aspects of a person's life, such as financial records, private conversations, or personal photos. Unlike traditional crimes that are confined to specific locations, cybercrimes can occur at any time and in any place, contributing to a heightened sense of vulnerability.

2.4.3 Lack of Immediate Physical Evidence

Traditional crimes, such as theft, assault, or vandalism, typically involve tangible evidence that victims can see and report to authorities. In contrast, the intangible nature of cybercrime makes it difficult for victims to assess the full extent of the damage immediately. For example, if a person's computer is infected with malware, they may not realize the system is compromised until after their data is stolen or their device is damaged. Similarly, when a financial institution is breached, individuals may not know their accounts have been accessed until fraudulent transactions occur.

This lack of visible damage or clear signs of wrongdoing can delay the recognition of a cybercrime, leaving victims unaware of the extent of the harm they have suffered until it is too late. Furthermore, the process of recovery may involve complex technical measures, such as cleaning up malware, restoring lost data, or dealing with the consequences of data manipulation, actions that are not immediately understandable to someone who lacks technical expertise.

2.4.4 Complexity and Technical Jargon

Cybercrime often requires specialized knowledge to fully understand and address the issues that arise. From data breaches to ransomware and SQL injection attacks, the technical language used in cybercrime investigations can be overwhelming for victims who are not familiar with the intricacies of computer systems or digital security. This lack of understanding can leave victims feeling confused, frustrated, or even embarrassed, especially if they feel they were easily tricked by a scam or failed to take sufficient security precautions.

In comparison, victims of physical crimes generally do not need to understand technical details to seek justice or recovery. For example, a person whose car is stolen does not need to be an expert in automotive systems or mechanics to report the crime, whereas a victim of cybercrime may need to navigate a labyrinth of complex processes, from identifying the source of an attack to restoring compromised data or securing their network.

2.4.5 Global and Cross-Jurisdictional Nature of Cybercrime

Another distinguishing feature of cybercrime is its global scope. While traditional crimes typically occur within a specific geographic area and fall under the jurisdiction of local or national law enforcement agencies, cybercrimes can occur anywhere in the world and affect victims in multiple countries. This creates significant jurisdictional challenges for both victims and law enforcement.

For example, if a victim is defrauded by a cybercriminal operating from another country, they may face significant barriers to getting justice, as the crime crosses international borders and may not fall under the jurisdiction of the victim's local authorities. This can result in delays, complications, and a sense of helplessness for victims who feel their case is not being prioritized or taken seriously.

2.4.6 Financial and Practical Consequences

Finally, victims of cybercrime may face unique financial and practical consequences. In traditional crimes like theft or burglary, victims generally have a clear understanding of what was taken (e.g., money, jewelry, electronics), and the process of restitution or insurance claims is usually straightforward. In contrast, victims of cybercrime often face financial losses that are more difficult to quantify, such as identity theft, fraud, or the costs of restoring systems after a data breach or ransomware attack.

For businesses, the consequences of cybercrime can include lost revenue, damage to brand reputation, and operational disruptions that extend far beyond the initial financial loss. The cost of recovering from a cyberattack can be significant, involving legal fees, the hiring of cybersecurity professionals, and extensive customer service efforts to restore trust and reputation.

2.5 Chapter Summary

In the modern digital landscape, cybercrime represents a significant and evolving threat that affects individuals, organizations, and governments across the globe. As we have explored throughout this document, cybercrime encompasses a wide range of illicit activities, from hacking and identity theft to cyberbullying and ransomware attacks. The anonymity of cybercriminals, the complex and global nature of their actions, and the emotional, financial, and technical impacts on victims distinguish cybercrime from traditional crimes, presenting unique challenges to both victims and law enforcement.

The rapid advancements in technology have amplified the scale and sophistication of cybercriminal activities, and as digital platforms become increasingly ingrained in daily life, these threats will likely continue to grow. However, understanding the various types of cybercrimes, the methodologies used by perpetrators, and the legal frameworks that exist to combat them is essential for mitigating the risks and providing effective responses.

Equally important are the victim support services available to those affected by cybercrime. These services, which include legal assistance, psychological support, identity recovery, and technical help, offer a holistic approach to helping victims recover and protect themselves from further harm. Despite the challenges of anonymity, complexity, and cross-jurisdictional issues, these services play a crucial role in guiding victims through the recovery process, advocating for stronger laws, and raising awareness about the importance of cybersecurity.

As the digital world continues to evolve, it is imperative for individuals, organizations, and governments to stay informed about the risks posed by cybercrime. By implementing strong security measures, understanding the impact of cybercrimes, and supporting victims, we can work together to build a safer and more secure digital environment. Furthermore, through continued advocacy, education, and international cooperation, we can better address the growing problem of cybercrime, ensuring that the victims of today are empowered to protect themselves and those of tomorrow.

Chapter 3
Understanding Laws and Legislation

Laws and legislation form the bedrock of any organized society, establishing the rules that govern behavior, protect rights, and ensure justice. They provide a structured framework within which individuals and organizations must operate, facilitating the resolution of disputes and the maintenance of public order. In an increasingly digital world, the complexity of crafting and enforcing laws has grown significantly, particularly in areas related to cybercrime, data privacy, and online consumer protection. As technology evolves, so too must the legal frameworks that regulate it, posing significant challenges to lawmakers and legal practitioners alike.

3.1 Introduction

For students of criminology, law, computer science, and cybersecurity, a comprehensive understanding of how laws and legislation are created, modified, and enforced is essential. Such knowledge not only aids in navigating the legal landscape but also empowers individuals to contribute effectively to policy-making processes and law enforcement strategies. This chapter provides a detailed exploration of the nature of laws and legislation, the processes involved in their creation and evolution, and the mechanisms of enforcement across various legal systems. Additionally, it offers a comparative analysis of legal frameworks in different countries, highlighting how nations balance the need for security, privacy, and consumer protection in the digital age.

By examining both national and international approaches to digital privacy, online consumer protection, and tech-facilitated crime, this chapter sets the stage for a deeper exploration of the challenges and opportunities presented by cybercrime and cybersecurity in the subsequent chapters.

M. K. A. Lukings et al., *Understanding Cybercrime Victim Services*, Progress in IS,
https://doi.org/10.1007/978-3-032-13273-4_3

3.2 Defining Laws and Legislation

Laws and legislation are fundamental components of any legal system, providing the formal rules and processes through which societies regulate behavior, protect rights, and uphold justice. Understanding the distinction between these two concepts is essential for analyzing how legal frameworks are developed, interpreted, and enforced.

3.2.1 What are Laws?

Laws are formal rules established by governing bodies to regulate human behavior within a society, ensuring order, justice, and the protection of individual rights. They serve as the foundation of legal systems, delineating what is considered permissible and impermissible conduct and setting out the consequences for violations. The authority of laws derives from various sources, including constitutions, statutes, judicial decisions, and customary practices, depending on the legal system in question. For a rule to be considered a law, it must not only be formally enacted but also enforceable by the state through institutions such as courts, law enforcement agencies, and regulatory bodies. Without enforceability, laws would lack the capacity to influence behavior and uphold social order effectively.

Laws perform multiple functions within a society, ranging from protecting individual and property rights to resolving disputes and maintaining public safety. By providing a predictable and structured framework for resolving conflicts, laws help build trust and stability, which are essential for both social and economic development. Furthermore, laws often embody the moral and ethical values of a society, promoting fairness, equity, and justice. For instance, anti-discrimination laws reflect societal commitments to equality and human dignity, while environmental regulations express a collective responsibility towards sustainable development.

Types of Laws:

Laws can be categorized into several broad types, each serving distinct functions and addressing different aspects of societal relations:

- **Criminal Law:**

  Focuses on offenses against the state or society as a whole, including crimes such as theft, assault, murder, and cybercrime. Its primary objective is to deter and penalize offenders while protecting public order and safety. Criminal laws prescribe punishments such as fines, imprisonment, and community service, with the severity of penalties often reflecting the gravity of the offense. The presumption of innocence, the right to a fair trial, and protections against self-incrimination are fundamental principles that underpin criminal law in most democratic societies.
- **Civil Law:**

Deals with disputes between private parties, including individuals, organizations, and businesses. Civil law covers a broad spectrum of issues, such as contractual disagreements, property disputes, family law matters, and torts (civil wrongs causing harm, such as defamation or negligence). Unlike criminal law, which focuses on punishment, civil law aims to provide remedies to those who have suffered harm, typically through monetary compensation or specific performance (fulfillment of contractual obligations). Civil law systems, prevalent in countries like France and Germany, are characterized by comprehensive legal codes that provide detailed guidance on various legal matters.

- **Administrative Law:**

  Governs the actions of government agencies and ensures they act within their legal authority. It establishes the processes for rulemaking, adjudication, and enforcement of regulations affecting areas such as immigration, environmental protection, healthcare, and business licensing. Administrative law also provides mechanisms for individuals to challenge government actions perceived as unlawful or arbitrary, typically through appeals or judicial review. For instance, environmental regulations may limit emissions from factories to protect public health and natural resources, while immigration rules control the entry and stay of non-citizens.

- **International Law**

  Consists of rules and principles that govern relations between sovereign states and international entities, encompassing treaties, conventions, customary practices, and principles of international comity. International law addresses issues such as human rights, trade, environmental protection, and armed conflict, seeking to promote cooperation and resolve disputes peacefully. While international law lacks centralized enforcement mechanisms, compliance is encouraged through diplomatic measures, economic sanctions, and, in some cases, adjudication by international courts, such as the International Court of Justice (ICJ) or the International Criminal Court (ICC).

Understanding the distinction between these types of laws is crucial for analyzing how different legal systems operate and how various forms of conduct are regulated and sanctioned. This differentiation also helps clarify the roles of different branches of government, legislative, executive, and judicial, in lawmaking and enforcement.

3.2.2 *What is Legislation?*

Legislation refers to the process by which statutory laws are proposed, debated, enacted, and codified by legislative bodies such as parliaments or congresses. It represents the formal mechanism through which societal norms, values, and policies are transformed into binding legal rules. Unlike common law, which evolves through judicial decisions and interpretations, legislation is characterized by its deliberate and proactive approach to lawmaking. Through legislation, elected representatives articulate and address specific policy issues, ranging from criminal justice and environmental regulation to economic policy and human rights.

Legislation is essential for democratic governance as it ensures that laws reflect the will and needs of the population. The legislative process involves multiple stages, including proposal, committee review, public debate, voting, and executive approval, allowing for comprehensive scrutiny and public participation. This process not only enhances the legitimacy of laws but also promotes transparency and accountability in government decision-making.

Key Components of Legislation:

Legislation encompasses several key components, each serving a distinct function within the legal system:

- **Statutes:**
  Formal written laws enacted by legislative bodies to address a wide range of issues, from criminal justice to environmental regulation. Statutes are often comprehensive and detailed, specifying the rights and duties of individuals, the powers of government agencies, and the penalties for non-compliance. For example, the Civil Rights Act of 1964 in the United States explicitly prohibits discrimination based on race, color, religion, sex, or national origin, reflecting societal commitments to equality and justice.
- **Regulations:**
  Detailed administrative rules created by governmental agencies to implement and enforce statutes effectively. Regulations translate the broad mandates of statutes into specific requirements and procedures that must be followed by individuals, businesses, and organizations. For instance, environmental regulations under the Clean Air Act in the U.S. specify permissible levels of emissions for industries, enforcement mechanisms, and penalties for violations. Regulations ensure that statutory laws are applied consistently and effectively across different contexts.
- **Ordinances:**
  Local laws enacted by municipal governments to address community-specific issues such as zoning, public safety, sanitation, and noise control. Ordinances enable local governments to respond to unique challenges and priorities within their jurisdictions, allowing for more targeted and flexible regulation. For example, a city may adopt ordinances to regulate short-term rentals, manage traffic congestion, or impose curfews to maintain public order.

Types of Legislative Systems:

Legislative systems can vary significantly across different countries, reflecting diverse political structures and traditions:

- **Unicameral Systems:**
  Consist of a single legislative chamber responsible for drafting, debating, and enacting laws. This system is often seen in smaller or more centralized countries,

such as Sweden or New Zealand, where a single chamber can efficiently manage legislative responsibilities.

- **Bicameral Systems:**
  Feature two legislative chambers, typically an upper house (e.g., the Senate) and a lower house (e.g., the House of Representatives), that must both approve proposed legislation. Bicameralism is designed to provide checks and balances, ensuring that laws are thoroughly reviewed and that different interests are represented.
- **Federal Systems:**
  Distribute legislative authority between national and subnational governments (states or provinces), allowing each level to enact laws within its jurisdiction. This system is seen in countries like the United States, Germany, and Canada, where state or provincial legislatures can address local issues while the national legislature manages broader policy areas.

Challenges and Considerations in Legislation:

Effective legislation must strike a balance between clarity and flexibility. Overly rigid statutes can quickly become outdated in fast-evolving fields such as technology and cybersecurity, while vague laws can lead to inconsistent enforcement and judicial interpretation. Additionally, the increasing complexity of modern societies requires legislators to navigate a wide array of competing interests, from business and environmental concerns to civil liberties and national security.

Understanding legislation's role and the legislative process is crucial for analyzing how legal systems adapt to societal changes and emerging challenges, particularly in areas like digital privacy, cybercrime, and international cooperation. This foundation is essential for exploring more specialized areas of law in subsequent chapters.

3.3 The Process of Creating Laws and Legislation

The process of creating laws and legislation is a structured and multi-stage procedure designed to transform policy ideas into binding legal rules. This process ensures that proposed laws are thoroughly examined, debated, and legitimized before being enacted, balancing the need for effective governance with democratic principles and public accountability.

3.3.1 The Legislative Process

The legislative process is a structured sequence of steps that transforms policy ideas into statutory laws. While the specifics of the legislative process vary across different legal systems, the core stages generally include a series of well-defined steps designed to ensure thorough examination, debate, and legitimacy of proposed laws. These stages are crucial for balancing diverse interests, preventing arbitrary lawmaking, and upholding democratic principles. The following is an in-depth look at each stage of the legislative process:

Stage One: Proposal

Legislation is typically introduced as a bill by a member of the legislative body, such as a parliamentarian or congressperson. Bills can originate from various sources, including elected representatives responding to constituents' demands, the executive branch proposing policies to address national priorities, or through public initiatives and referenda in countries that permit direct democracy mechanisms. In some jurisdictions, interest groups and advocacy organizations also play a significant role in shaping legislative proposals by conducting research, drafting bills, and lobbying lawmakers. The initial proposal must clearly outline the purpose, scope, and anticipated impact of the legislation to gain support and proceed to the next stage.

Stage Two: Committee Review

Once introduced, the bill is referred to a specialized committee that examines its provisions in detail. Committees, which consist of legislators with expertise in relevant policy areas, conduct hearings to gather input from experts, stakeholders, and the public. This stage often includes consultations with legal scholars, industry representatives, advocacy groups, and other stakeholders to assess the bill's potential implications and feasibility. Committee members can propose amendments to refine the bill, address ambiguities, and incorporate expert recommendations. The committee's report, which includes a summary of findings and suggested changes, is crucial in shaping the bill's content before it returns to the full legislative body for further consideration.

Stage Three: Debate.

Following the committee review, the bill proceeds to the floor of the legislative body for open debate. During this stage, legislators engage in discussions to assess the bill's merits, its alignment with national priorities, and its potential social, economic, and legal impacts. Debates may be highly contentious, especially for bills addressing divisive issues such as privacy rights, cybersecurity measures, or criminal justice reforms. Legislators can propose additional amendments during this stage, seeking to build broader support or address specific concerns. The quality and depth of these debates are critical, as they allow elected representatives to voice the interests of their constituents and scrutinize the proposed legislation comprehensively.

Stage Four: Voting.

After the debate concludes, the bill is put to a vote in the legislative chambers. The voting process varies based on the type of bill and the legislative system in place. For standard bills, a simple majority is typically required to pass. However, for constitutional amendments, budget bills, or significant legal reforms, some jurisdictions mandate a supermajority vote. Voting can be conducted through different methods, such as voice votes, roll-call votes, or electronic systems, ensuring transparency and accountability. If the bill fails to secure the necessary votes, it may be revised or reintroduced in a subsequent session.

Stage Five: Executive Approval.

Once a bill is approved by the legislative body, it is forwarded to the head of state, such as a president, monarch, or governor, for final consent. The executive has several options: sign the bill into law, veto it, or return it with recommendations for modifications. In systems with a strong separation of powers, a vetoed bill can often be overridden by a supermajority vote in the legislature. Some jurisdictions also allow the executive to exercise a line-item veto, permitting them to reject specific provisions of a bill without discarding the entire document. This stage serves as an additional check to ensure that legislation is both constitutionally sound and aligned with the broader policy agenda of the executive branch.

Stage Six: Enactment.

If the executive approves the bill, it is formally enacted into law and published in official gazettes or legal repositories, making it accessible to the public. The enactment stage involves specifying the date when the law will come into effect, which can be immediate or delayed to allow sufficient time for implementation measures, such as establishing regulatory bodies, issuing administrative guidelines, or conducting public awareness campaigns. In some cases, the enactment includes transitional provisions to manage the shift from previous legal frameworks smoothly. The publication of the law ensures transparency and enables individuals and organizations to familiarize themselves with the new legal requirements.

3.3.2 The Role of Public Participation in Legislation

Public participation plays a crucial role in the legislative process by enhancing transparency, accountability, and the democratic legitimacy of laws. In many democratic systems, the public can influence legislation directly through mechanisms such as public consultations, petitions, and referenda, or indirectly by communicating with their elected representatives. Public hearings, open committee meetings, and the solicitation of feedback from stakeholders enable citizens, advocacy groups, and industry representatives to express their views on proposed legislation, identify potential impacts, and suggest amendments. This input can significantly shape the content and direction of laws, particularly on issues of broad public concern such as environmental protection, data privacy, and consumer rights.

In some jurisdictions, e-democracy tools such as online petitions, digital platforms for public comment, and participatory budgeting processes have further expanded opportunities for public involvement in lawmaking. For example, the European

Union's European Citizens' Initiative allows citizens to propose legislative actions if they gather a sufficient number of signatures across member states. Such mechanisms not only enhance the responsiveness of legislative bodies but also help build public trust and compliance with the law.

3.3.3 Challenges in the Legislative Process

The legislative process faces several challenges that can hinder its effectiveness and responsiveness to emerging issues. One significant challenge is legislative gridlock, which occurs when political polarization or institutional conflicts prevent the passage of essential laws. Gridlock can delay responses to urgent issues such as cybersecurity threats, public health crises, and financial regulation, leaving gaps in the legal framework.

Another challenge is the influence of special interest groups and lobbying, which can result in legislation that prioritizes corporate or partisan interests over the public good. While lobbying is a legitimate part of the democratic process, the lack of transparency in lobbying activities can lead to perceptions of corruption and erode public trust in legislative institutions.

Additionally, the growing complexity of modern societies and the rapid pace of technological change often outstrip the capacity of legislative bodies to craft timely and effective laws. The technical and specialized nature of issues such as artificial intelligence regulation, data privacy, and digital currencies requires expertise that many legislators may lack, necessitating greater reliance on experts and regulatory agencies.

In summary, while the legislative process is fundamental to democratic governance, addressing these challenges is essential for ensuring that laws are responsive, fair, and capable of addressing the evolving needs of society.

3.4 Development and Evolution of Laws

The development and evolution of laws are continuous processes that enable legal systems to adapt to changing societal values, technological advancements, and emerging challenges. Through mechanisms such as amendments, repeals, and judicial interpretations, laws are refined and updated to remain relevant, just, and effective in addressing contemporary issues. This adaptability is crucial for ensuring that legal frameworks can adequately protect individual rights, promote social justice, and maintain public order in an ever-changing world.

3.4.1 Amendments and Repeals

Laws must evolve to address changing societal needs, emerging technologies, and new types of criminal behavior. Amendments modify existing laws to clarify, expand, or restrict their scope, while repeals eliminate outdated or unjust laws. For example, the rise of the internet necessitated amendments to criminal codes worldwide to include cybercrimes such as hacking, identity theft, and online fraud. Similarly, evolving societal attitudes towards issues like same-sex marriage and cannabis legalization have led to significant legislative amendments in many countries.

Amendments can be initiated by the legislature, the executive, or through public referenda, depending on the legal framework. In parliamentary systems, the introduction of amendment bills follows the same legislative process as new laws, requiring debate, committee review, and approval by both legislative chambers. In federal systems, amendments to the constitution often require a more rigorous process, such as supermajority approval in both federal and state legislatures or a national referendum. The flexibility to amend and repeal laws is essential for maintaining the relevance and fairness of the legal system, allowing it to adapt to new societal norms, technological developments, and emerging threats.

3.4.2 Judicial Interpretation and Precedents

Judicial interpretation plays a fundamental role in the evolution of laws, particularly in common law systems, where courts not only apply statutes but also interpret and, in some cases, expand upon them through case law and judicial precedents. When courts interpret statutes, they clarify ambiguities, fill gaps, and adapt legal principles to new and unforeseen circumstances. This interpretative function allows laws to evolve incrementally in response to societal changes without requiring frequent legislative amendments.

For instance, judicial interpretations of privacy rights in the context of digital surveillance and data collection have significantly influenced the application of constitutional protections against unreasonable searches and seizures in countries like the United States. Landmark cases such as Riley v. California (2014), in which the U.S. Supreme Court ruled that law enforcement must obtain a warrant to search digital information on a cell phone, have extended traditional privacy rights to new technologies. Similarly, courts in European Union member states have played a crucial role in interpreting the General Data Protection Regulation (GDPR), providing clarity on data subject rights, consent requirements, and the scope of cross-border data transfers.

Precedents set by higher courts serve as binding authority on lower courts, ensuring consistency and predictability in the application of laws. However, judicial precedents are not static; higher courts can overturn previous decisions to reflect evolving societal values, emerging threats, or new understandings of constitutional principles. For example, the U.S. Supreme Court's decision in Obergefell v. Hodges (2015), which legalized same-sex marriage nationwide, overturned previous precedents that upheld restrictions on marriage rights.

In civil law systems, where judicial decisions do not carry the same precedential weight, courts still influence the evolution of laws through interpretive rulings that clarify statutory provisions. Constitutional courts, in particular, play a vital role by reviewing the constitutionality of legislation and administrative actions, effectively shaping the scope and application of laws. For example, the German Federal Constitutional Court has issued landmark rulings on data retention and privacy that have prompted legislative reforms at both the national and EU levels.

The balance between legislative intent and judicial interpretation is a dynamic aspect of legal evolution. Courts must interpret laws in a manner that respects legislative intent while ensuring that legal principles remain relevant and capable of addressing contemporary challenges. Understanding the role of judicial interpretation is essential for analyzing how laws adapt to new contexts without requiring constant legislative intervention.

3.4.3 The Impact of International Law and Treaties

International law and treaties play a significant role in the evolution of national legal systems, particularly in areas that require cross-border cooperation, such as trade, environmental protection, human rights, and cybercrime. By ratifying international treaties, countries commit to aligning their national laws with international standards, often necessitating legislative reforms and amendments to domestic statutes. This process not only harmonizes laws across jurisdictions but also addresses gaps in national legislation that may be exploited by transnational actors.

For instance, the Budapest Convention on Cybercrime, the first international treaty aimed at addressing cybercrime, has significantly influenced national laws by providing a legal framework for combating online threats such as hacking, data breaches, and digital fraud. Signatories to the Convention are required to adopt substantive and procedural laws that facilitate cross-border investigations, mutual legal assistance, and extradition of cybercriminals. Many European and non-European countries have amended their national criminal codes to incorporate provisions aligned with the Convention, thereby enhancing their ability to combat transnational cybercrime effectively.

Similarly, international human rights treaties, such as the International Covenant on Civil and Political Rights (ICCPR) and the Convention on the Elimination of All Forms of Discrimination Against Women (CEDAW), have prompted legislative reforms aimed at eliminating discriminatory practices, ensuring due process rights, and protecting freedoms of expression, assembly, and privacy. For example, numerous countries have introduced anti-discrimination laws, domestic violence protections, and legal recognition of gender rights as part of their obligations under international human rights treaties.

Trade agreements also play a crucial role in shaping national laws, particularly in areas such as intellectual property, data protection, and digital commerce. For example, the Comprehensive and Progressive Agreement for Trans-Pacific Partnership (CPTPP) includes provisions that require member countries to strengthen intellectual property protections, ensure free cross-border data flows, and adopt robust cybersecurity measures. Compliance with these provisions often necessitates amendments to national intellectual property laws, privacy regulations, and cybersecurity frameworks, demonstrating the significant impact of international agreements on domestic legislation.

The influence of international law is particularly pronounced in the European Union, where member states are required to incorporate EU directives and regulations into their national legal systems. Directives such as the General Data Protection Regulation (GDPR) and the Directive on Security of Network and Information Systems (NIS Directive) have led to comprehensive legislative reforms across member states, setting high standards for data protection, cybersecurity, and consumer rights.

However, the integration of international law into national legal systems is not without challenges. Sovereignty concerns, conflicts between international obligations and domestic priorities, and variations in legal traditions can complicate the process of implementing international treaties. Additionally, the lack of effective enforcement mechanisms for international law can limit its impact, particularly in addressing human rights violations and environmental crimes.

In summary, the impact of international law and treaties on the evolution of national legal systems highlights the growing interdependence of national and international legal frameworks. As globalization continues to blur the boundaries between domestic and international law, understanding the mechanisms through which international agreements influence national legislation is essential for analyzing the development and evolution of laws in a globalized world.

3.5 Enforcement of Laws

The enforcement of laws is a crucial aspect of any legal system, ensuring that legal rules are upheld and that individuals and organizations comply with their obligations. This process involves a coordinated effort by law enforcement agencies, regulatory bodies, and the judiciary to investigate violations, prosecute offenders, and impose appropriate sanctions to maintain public order and justice.

3.5.1 Law Enforcement Agencies

The enforcement of laws is a crucial component of any legal system, ensuring that legal rules are upheld, violations are investigated, and offenders are prosecuted and sanctioned appropriately. Effective law enforcement not only maintains public order and safety but also reinforces trust in the legal system by demonstrating that laws are applied fairly and consistently. Law enforcement agencies operate at various levels, local, national, and international, each playing a distinct role in investigating crimes, ensuring compliance with regulations, and administering justice. The complexity of modern law enforcement has grown significantly with the rise of transnational threats such as cybercrime, terrorism, and human trafficking, necessitating enhanced coordination and resource-sharing across jurisdictions.

The key institutions involved in law enforcement include the police, regulatory bodies, and the judiciary, each with specific responsibilities and functions. Effective law enforcement requires not only adequate resources and specialized expertise but also robust mechanisms for inter-agency cooperation, information sharing, and cross-border collaboration, particularly in dealing with sophisticated and transnational crimes like cybercrime, financial fraud, and organized crime.

3.5.2 Challenges in Law Enforcement

Law enforcement agencies face a wide array of challenges that complicate their ability to investigate and prosecute crimes effectively. One of the most significant challenges is the rapid advancement of technology, which has transformed both the nature of crime and the methods available for law enforcement. Cybercrime, in particular, presents unique difficulties due to the anonymity of perpetrators, jurisdictional complexities, and the technical sophistication required for investigations. Crimes such as hacking, ransomware attacks, and online fraud often span multiple countries, necessitating cross-border cooperation and harmonization of legal frameworks. The increasing use of encryption and anonymization tools further complicates evidence collection and surveillance, creating a "going dark" problem where law enforcement agencies are unable to access critical information even with legal authorization.

Another significant challenge is the limited resources and funding available to many law enforcement agencies, particularly at the local level. Investigating complex financial crimes, cyber incidents, and human trafficking cases often requires specialized expertise, advanced forensic tools, and significant manpower, which are frequently beyond the reach of underfunded agencies. Budget constraints can also impact training programs, reducing the ability of officers to stay updated on the latest investigative techniques and legal developments.

Jurisdictional conflicts pose additional challenges, particularly for transnational crimes that involve multiple countries with different legal standards and enforcement capabilities. The lack of a unified international framework for addressing cybercrime complicates efforts to investigate, apprehend, and prosecute offenders who exploit jurisdictional gaps. Mutual legal assistance treaties (MLATs) and organizations such as Interpol and Europol play critical roles in facilitating cross-border investigations, but bureaucratic delays and differences in privacy standards often hinder timely cooperation.

Ethical dilemmas and public scrutiny also challenge law enforcement agencies, particularly regarding surveillance practices, data privacy, and the use of emerging technologies such as facial recognition and artificial intelligence. Balancing the need for effective crime prevention with the protection of individual rights and civil liberties is a contentious issue, requiring clear legal standards, transparency, and oversight mechanisms. Allegations of bias in policing, excessive use of force, and misuse of surveillance technologies have further eroded public trust in law enforcement in many countries, underscoring the need for accountability and reform.

Additionally, the rise of misinformation and digital disinformation campaigns has created new challenges for law enforcement. Coordinated misinformation campaigns aimed at disrupting elections, inciting violence, or undermining public trust in institutions require sophisticated capabilities to detect, attribute, and counter. The role of social media platforms and the need for regulatory frameworks that mandate transparency and accountability in online content moderation have become central issues in this context.

3.5.3 Enhancing Law Enforcement Capabilities

Addressing the challenges faced by law enforcement requires a multifaceted approach that includes increasing resources, enhancing training, fostering interagency cooperation, and leveraging technology effectively. One of the primary strategies for enhancing law enforcement capabilities is investing in specialized units and training programs focused on emerging threats such as cybercrime, financial crimes, and human trafficking. For instance, the establishment of dedicated cybercrime units within national police forces, equipped with digital forensics experts and cutting-edge tools, has proven effective in investigating online threats and coordinating responses to cyber incidents.

Strengthening international cooperation is also crucial for addressing transnational crimes. Participation in international organizations such as Interpol, the Financial Action Task Force (FATF), and the European Union Agency for Law Enforcement Cooperation (Europol) facilitates information sharing, joint investigations, and capacity-building initiatives. For example, Europol's European Cybercrime Centre (EC3) provides operational support to EU member states in combating cybercrime, coordinating intelligence, and disseminating best practices for digital investigations.

Legislative reforms aimed at harmonizing national laws with international standards can also enhance law enforcement capabilities. Adopting comprehensive data protection and cybercrime laws that comply with instruments such as the Budapest

Convention on Cybercrime enables countries to streamline cross-border investigations and reduce jurisdictional conflicts. Establishing clear legal standards for data retention, encryption, and surveillance can help law enforcement agencies access critical evidence while ensuring respect for privacy rights.

Technology plays a pivotal role in enhancing law enforcement effectiveness. The integration of artificial intelligence (AI) for predictive policing, big data analytics for detecting financial crimes, and blockchain for ensuring evidence integrity has opened new avenues for combating complex crimes. AI-driven tools that analyze large datasets can help identify patterns, predict hotspots for crime, and optimize resource allocation. However, the use of AI and predictive policing must be governed by robust ethical guidelines to prevent biases, ensure transparency, and protect civil liberties.

Public-private partnerships have emerged as a valuable strategy for enhancing law enforcement capabilities. Collaboration between law enforcement agencies and technology companies, financial institutions, and cybersecurity firms enables more effective responses to cyber threats, financial fraud, and online extremism. Initiatives such as the Cybersecurity Information Sharing Act (CISA) in the United States encourage information sharing between the private sector and government agencies, enhancing situational awareness and enabling proactive threat mitigation.

Enhancing accountability and public trust is also essential for effective law enforcement. Implementing body-worn cameras, establishing independent oversight bodies, and adopting transparency measures in law enforcement practices can help restore public confidence and reduce perceptions of bias and abuse of power. Public trust is particularly critical in areas such as counter-terrorism and cybercrime, where cooperation with communities and businesses is essential for intelligence gathering and threat prevention.

In conclusion, enhancing law enforcement capabilities in the face of evolving challenges requires a holistic approach that integrates resources, technology, international cooperation, and accountability. As threats continue to evolve, law enforcement agencies must adapt by embracing new tools and strategies while ensuring that their actions align with legal standards and respect for fundamental rights. Understanding these dynamics is essential for developing effective policies and practices to strengthen law enforcement in the digital age.

3.6 How Laws Are Created, Altered, and Enforced: A Comparative Perspective

The ways in which laws are created, altered, and enforced can vary significantly across different countries, reflecting diverse legal traditions, political systems, and societal priorities. A comparative perspective provides valuable insights into how various nations approach the challenges of lawmaking, adaptation to new issues, and the enforcement of legal norms, particularly in the context of digital privacy, online consumer protection, and tech-facilitated crime.

3.6.1 Canada

Canada has developed a comprehensive and multifaceted legal framework to address digital privacy, online consumer protection, and tech-facilitated crime, reflecting its commitment to protecting individual rights and maintaining a secure digital environment. This framework is characterized by a combination of federal and provincial laws, which operate within a constitutional monarchy and parliamentary democracy, ensuring both national coherence and flexibility to address regional differences.

Digital Privacy Laws.

The Personal Information Protection and Electronic Documents Act (PIPEDA) serves as the cornerstone of Canada's digital privacy regime. Enacted in 2000 and significantly amended by the Digital Privacy Act (2015), PIPEDA regulates how private sector organizations collect, use, and disclose personal information during commercial activities. It mandates organizations to obtain meaningful consent before collecting personal data, limit data collection to what is necessary, and implement adequate security safeguards to protect the data. The 2015 amendments introduced mandatory data breach notification requirements, compelling organizations to inform both affected individuals and the Office of the Privacy Commissioner of Canada (OPC) of breaches that pose a "real risk of significant harm." This framework not only enhances transparency and accountability but also aligns Canada's privacy standards with international best practices, facilitating data flows with jurisdictions that have stringent privacy laws, such as the European Union.

Additionally, provincial privacy laws such as the Personal Information Protection Act (PIPA) in Alberta and British Columbia, and the Act Respecting the Protection of Personal Information in the Private Sector in Quebec, complement PIPEDA by addressing region-specific privacy concerns. These laws provide enhanced protections, particularly in areas like employee privacy and consent requirements, illustrating how Canada's federal system enables tailored privacy safeguards.

Online Consumer Protection Laws.

Canada has implemented a robust set of laws to protect consumers in the digital marketplace, focusing on transparency, fairness, and security. Canada's Anti-Spam Legislation (CASL), which came into effect in 2014, is one of the strictest anti-spam laws globally. CASL regulates the dissemination of commercial electronic messages by requiring explicit consent from recipients, clear sender identification, and an easy-to-use unsubscribe mechanism. It also prohibits the installation of software without user consent, targeting practices like spyware and malware distribution. The penalties for non-compliance are substantial, with fines reaching up to $ten million for organizations and $one million for individuals, underscoring the seriousness with which Canada approaches online threats.

The Competition Act further strengthens consumer protection by prohibiting misleading advertising, deceptive marketing practices, and false or misleading representations in online and offline marketplaces. It grants the Competition Bureau the authority to investigate and take action against businesses engaging in deceptive practices, such as fake online reviews, false discounts, and bait-and-switch tactics. The Bureau's ability to impose administrative monetary penalties (AMPs) serves as a deterrent against violations, ensuring a fair digital marketplace.

In addition to these federal measures, provincial consumer protection laws enhance online shopping safeguards. For instance, Ontario's Consumer Protection Act mandates clear disclosure of terms and conditions for online contracts, a cooling-off period for certain online purchases, and protection against unfair practices.

Tech-Facilitated Crime Laws.

Canada's approach to tech-facilitated crime is anchored in the Criminal Code, which includes comprehensive provisions to address a wide range of cybercrimes. Amendments to the Criminal Code under Bill C-13 (Protecting Canadians from Online Crime Act) introduced specific offenses targeting cyberbullying, nonconsensual distribution of intimate images, and online harassment. These provisions empower law enforcement agencies to request preservation orders for electronic evidence and streamline the process for obtaining warrants to investigate cybercrimes.

Cybersecurity is further reinforced by the Security of Information Act, which addresses espionage, unauthorized access to classified information, and cyber intrusions targeting critical infrastructure. This Act includes provisions for prosecuting individuals or entities that compromise national security through cyber means.

To enforce these laws, Canada employs a collaborative approach between federal and provincial law enforcement agencies. The Royal Canadian Mounted Police (RCMP), through its National Cybercrime Coordination Unit (NC3), leads federal efforts to combat cybercrime, focusing on intelligence sharing, public awareness campaigns, and coordination with international partners. The RCMP's collaboration with provincial police forces and regulatory bodies such as the Canadian Security Intelligence Service (CSIS) and the Communications Security Establishment (CSE) enhances Canada's capacity to respond to complex cyber threats effectively.

Canada's active participation in international initiatives, such as the Budapest Convention on Cybercrime and partnerships within the Five Eyes intelligence alliance, highlights its commitment to addressing transnational cyber threats. These collaborations facilitate cross-border information sharing and joint operations, enabling Canada to respond swiftly to cyber incidents that span multiple jurisdictions.

Challenges and Future Directions.

Despite its comprehensive legal framework, Canada faces ongoing challenges in addressing tech-facilitated crime, particularly in areas such as encryption, anonymity, and cross-border jurisdictional issues. The growing use of encrypted communication by cybercriminals complicates investigations, limiting law enforcement's ability to intercept and access critical evidence. The lack of mandatory data retention laws further hampers efforts to preserve digital evidence for investigations.

In response, Canada is exploring new legislative measures, including a proposed update to PIPEDA, known as Bill C-27 (the Digital Charter Implementation Act), which seeks to enhance privacy rights, introduce new data portability provisions, and create a Privacy Tribunal to handle enforcement more efficiently. Additionally, ongoing discussions about regulating artificial intelligence and expanding the scope of cybersecurity laws indicate a proactive approach to evolving threats.

Overall, Canada's legal framework reflects a balanced approach that seeks to protect individual privacy rights while maintaining robust mechanisms for consumer protection and combating tech-facilitated crime. By continuously updating its laws to address emerging challenges, Canada demonstrates a commitment to fostering a secure, fair, and transparent digital environment.

3.6.2 United States

The United States has developed a complex but comprehensive legal framework for addressing digital privacy, online consumer protection, and tech-facilitated crime. This framework is characterized by a mix of federal and state laws, reflecting the federalist structure of the U.S. government. While this approach allows states to address specific regional concerns, it also leads to a fragmented legal landscape, particularly in the area of digital privacy. The absence of a single, overarching federal privacy law has resulted in a patchwork of regulations that vary significantly between states, complicating compliance for businesses operating nationwide.

Digital Privacy Laws.

Digital privacy in the United States is governed by a combination of state-level initiatives and sector-specific federal laws. The California Consumer Privacy Act (CCPA), enacted in 2018, is the most comprehensive state privacy law to date, granting California residents significant rights over their personal information. Under the CCPA, consumers have the right to know what personal information is being collected, request the deletion of their data, and opt-out of the sale of their information. Businesses covered by the CCPA are required to disclose their data practices transparently and provide mechanisms for consumers to exercise their rights. The law's enforcement by the California Attorney General includes penalties of up to $7500 per violation for intentional breaches, setting a high standard for data privacy in the United States.

Federally, digital privacy is regulated through a series of sector-specific laws rather than a comprehensive national statute. The Children's Online Privacy Protection Act (COPPA), for example, protects children's privacy by imposing strict requirements on websites and online services targeting children under the age of 13. COPPA mandates parental consent for data collection, limits data retention, and requires clear privacy policies, with enforcement by the Federal Trade Commission (FTC). In the healthcare sector, the Health Insurance Portability and Accountability Act (HIPAA) establishes standards for protecting sensitive patient information, mandating safeguards for data privacy and security.

The absence of a federal privacy law like the General Data Protection Regulation (GDPR) in the European Union has prompted other states to adopt their own privacy regulations, such as the Virginia Consumer Data Protection Act (VCDPA) and the Colorado Privacy Act (CPA). This evolving landscape suggests a growing momentum towards comprehensive federal privacy legislation, with several bills, including the American Data Privacy Protection Act (ADPPA), under consideration in Congress.

Online Consumer Protection Laws.

The United States has a well-established framework for online consumer protection, focusing on transparency, fairness, and security in digital transactions. The Federal Trade Commission Act (FTCA) serves as a cornerstone, empowering the FTC to investigate and take action against deceptive and unfair business practices. Under the FTCA, the FTC has pursued numerous enforcement actions against companies engaging in false advertising, data breaches, and other online scams. Notably, the FTC's authority extends to enforcing privacy promises made by businesses, such as those outlined in privacy policies, treating deceptive statements as violations of consumer rights.

The CAN-SPAM Act, passed in 2003, further strengthens consumer protection by regulating commercial email practices. It requires businesses to provide accurate header information, avoid misleading subject lines, and include a visible opt-out mechanism in all commercial emails. The law also prohibits the use of deceptive tactics to harvest email addresses or generate traffic through false pretenses. Violations of the CAN-SPAM Act can result in penalties of up to $43,792 per email, providing a strong deterrent against spam and phishing campaigns.

State laws complement these federal protections by addressing specific regional concerns and closing gaps in federal regulations. For example, the New York SHIELD Act imposes enhanced data security requirements and broadens the definition of personal information subject to protection. Similarly, the Massachusetts Data Security Regulation mandates encryption of personal data stored or transmitted electronically, illustrating how state initiatives enhance consumer protection in the absence of comprehensive federal regulations.

Tech-Facilitated Crime Laws.

The United States has developed an extensive legal framework to combat tech-facilitated crime, addressing challenges such as hacking, identity theft, and cyberstalking. The Computer Fraud and Abuse Act (CFAA), enacted in 1986, remains the primary federal statute for prosecuting unauthorized access to computer systems and data. The CFAA criminalizes a range of activities, from hacking and data breaches to the transmission of malware and denial-of-service attacks. It provides for both criminal penalties and civil remedies, allowing companies to sue hackers for damages. However, the CFAA has been criticized for its broad language, which has led to controversial prosecutions and calls for reform to clarify the distinction between criminal hacking and legitimate security research.

The Electronic Communications Privacy Act (ECPA) of 1986 extends protections to electronic communications, prohibiting unauthorized interception, access, and disclosure of communications stored by service providers. The ECPA's Stored Communications Act (SCA) component regulates access to emails and files stored on remote servers, requiring law enforcement to obtain warrants based on probable cause for most types of data. The Act, however, has been criticized for being outdated in addressing the complexities of cloud computing and modern digital communications, prompting legislative efforts to modernize its provisions.

To address cross-border cybercrime, the United States actively participates in international initiatives, including the Budapest Convention on Cybercrime. This treaty facilitates cooperation between member states in investigating and prosecuting cybercrimes that span multiple jurisdictions. Domestically, the Federal Bureau of Investigation (FBI) and the Department of Homeland Security (DHS) play critical roles in investigating cybercrimes, supported by specialized units such as the Internet Crime Complaint Center (IC3) and the Cybersecurity and Infrastructure Security Agency (CISA). These agencies focus on intelligence sharing, incident response, and public awareness campaigns to mitigate the impact of cyber threats.

Challenges and Future Directions.

Despite its comprehensive legal framework, the United States faces significant challenges in addressing tech-facilitated crime, particularly in areas like encryption, jurisdictional conflicts, and balancing privacy with national security. The widespread use of end-to-end encryption by technology companies has created "going dark" challenges for law enforcement, limiting their ability to access communications even with court orders. Additionally, the fragmented nature of U.S. privacy laws complicates compliance for businesses and enforcement for regulators, creating a strong impetus for a unified federal privacy law.

Emerging legislative efforts, such as the proposed EARN IT Act, which seeks to limit legal protections for tech companies that fail to combat child exploitation content effectively, reflect ongoing attempts to balance privacy rights with security imperatives. Similarly, debates around encryption backdoors and lawful access to encrypted communications underscore the tension between privacy advocates and law enforcement agencies.

Overall, the United States' legal framework for digital privacy, consumer protection, and tech-facilitated crime reflects a balance between protecting individual rights and ensuring national security. The dynamic interplay between federal and state laws allows for innovative approaches to emerging challenges, but also highlights the need for greater coherence and modernization of existing regulations.

3.6.3 China

China has developed a centralized and stringent legal framework for managing digital privacy, online consumer protection, and tech-facilitated crime, reflecting the broader approach of the Chinese government to governance and control. This framework is characterized by comprehensive national laws, strict data localization requirements, and extensive government surveillance capabilities. China's legal system, shaped by its one-party structure, prioritizes state security and social stability, often at the expense of individual privacy rights and freedoms. The centralized nature of lawmaking and enforcement allows for swift and decisive legal responses to emerging challenges, particularly in the digital realm.

Digital Privacy Laws.

China's approach to digital privacy is primarily governed by the Personal Information Protection Law (PIPL), which came into effect in 2021. Often compared to the General Data Protection Regulation (GDPR) in the European Union, the PIPL is China's first comprehensive privacy law, establishing a robust framework for protecting personal information. The PIPL mandates that organizations obtain explicit consent from users before collecting personal data and imposes strict requirements on data processors to ensure security. The law also grants individuals rights to access, correct, and delete their personal information, as well as the right to restrict or object to processing in certain circumstances.

One of the most significant aspects of the PIPL is its stringent data localization and cross-border data transfer requirements. It mandates that critical information infrastructure operators (CIIOs) and companies handling large amounts of personal data must store this data domestically. Cross-border transfers of personal data are subject to security assessments by the Cyberspace Administration of China (CAC), contractual safeguards, and in some cases, individual consent. Non-compliance with the PIPL can result in severe penalties, including fines of up to 5% of a company's global annual turnover or approximately $7.7 million, whichever is higher, alongside potential criminal liabilities for responsible individuals.

In addition to the PIPL, China's Cybersecurity Law of 2017 enhances government control over data and internet activities by requiring network operators to comply with security certification standards, store specific types of data within China, and submit to security reviews for network products and services. The law also mandates real-name registration for internet users, facilitating government monitoring of online activities. Combined, the PIPL and Cybersecurity Law form a comprehensive legal structure that emphasizes state security and control over data privacy.

Online Consumer Protection Laws.

China's online consumer protection framework is governed by the E-Commerce Law (2019) and the Consumer Rights Protection Law. The E-Commerce Law was introduced to address challenges posed by the rapid growth of online retail in China, which has become the world's largest e-commerce market. It establishes clear liabilities for e-commerce platforms concerning counterfeit goods, fraudulent activities, and consumer rights violations. Platforms like Alibaba, JD.com, and Pinduoduo are required to verify the authenticity of products sold and ensure that consumer complaints are addressed promptly. Failure to comply can result in substantial fines and restrictions on business operations.

The E-Commerce Law also includes provisions for protecting consumers' personal information, requiring online platforms to disclose data collection practices transparently and obtain user consent. Additionally, the law mandates that platforms must prevent deceptive practices such as fake reviews, false advertising, and manipulated search results. These measures aim to build consumer trust and ensure a level playing field in China's highly competitive e-commerce landscape.

The Consumer Rights Protection Law complements the E-Commerce Law by mandating accurate product descriptions, clear refund policies, and safeguards against unfair contractual terms. It empowers the State Administration for Market Regulation (SAMR) to conduct investigations, impose fines, and order corrective actions for non-compliance. The law's provisions are particularly relevant in the context of mobile payments and digital financial services, which have seen explosive growth in China.

Tech-Facilitated Crime Laws.

China has enacted a series of laws to combat tech-facilitated crime, focusing on both national security and public order. The Criminal Law of China includes provisions for hacking, online fraud, identity theft, and the dissemination of false information. Specific articles of the Criminal Law criminalize unauthorized access to computer networks, distribution of malicious software, and cyberattacks on critical infrastructure. Penalties for such offenses can range from fines to long-term imprisonment, depending on the severity and impact of the crime.

The Data Security Law (DSL), which took effect in 2021, further strengthens China's ability to manage data-related risks, particularly those that could affect national security. The DSL classifies data based on its importance to national security and the public interest, imposing heightened security requirements for critical and sensitive data. Companies handling such data are required to conduct periodic risk assessments, implement robust encryption measures, and report any data breaches to regulatory authorities promptly. The law also restricts the export of data deemed critical to national security, reinforcing China's data sovereignty agenda.

Law enforcement in China is centralized under the Ministry of Public Security (MPS), which has broad powers to monitor, investigate, and regulate online activities. The MPS collaborates closely with the People's Liberation Army (PLA) and the Ministry of State Security (MSS) to combat cyber espionage, foreign influence, and threats to national security. The use of advanced surveillance technologies, including facial recognition, artificial intelligence, and extensive internet censorship through the Great Firewall, illustrates the state's comprehensive approach to controlling the digital space. This centralized enforcement mechanism ensures that tech-facilitated crimes are dealt with swiftly but also raises significant concerns regarding privacy, censorship, and human rights.

Challenges and Future Directions.

Despite its comprehensive and stringent legal framework, China faces several challenges in balancing security and privacy, particularly concerning cross-border data flows and compliance with international standards. The stringent data localization requirements under the PIPL and the Cybersecurity Law have raised concerns among foreign businesses regarding compliance costs and operational complexities. Additionally, China's expansive surveillance practices and the lack of judicial independence in reviewing state actions limit the effectiveness of privacy protections provided by the PIPL, creating a significant trust deficit both domestically and internationally.

Looking forward, China's legal landscape is likely to evolve further with the introduction of more detailed regulations on emerging technologies such as artificial intelligence, blockchain, and autonomous systems. Draft regulations under consideration include provisions for AI ethics, data ownership rights, and expanded cybersecurity requirements for critical sectors. Additionally, the ongoing negotiations between China and other countries regarding data transfer mechanisms and compliance with international privacy standards suggest a potential shift towards more harmonized regulations.

Overall, China's legal framework for digital privacy, online consumer protection, and tech-facilitated crime reflects a state-centric approach that prioritizes national security and social stability. The combination of comprehensive laws, centralized enforcement, and advanced surveillance capabilities demonstrates the state's commitment to maintaining control over the digital environment, even as it navigates complex relationships with foreign businesses and international regulatory standards.

3.6.4 Germany

Germany has established a comprehensive and robust legal framework to address digital privacy, online consumer protection, and tech-facilitated crime, reflecting its commitment to protecting individual rights and ensuring a secure digital environment. As a federal republic with a strong tradition of civil law, Germany's legal system integrates national statutes with European Union regulations, providing a cohesive approach to emerging challenges in the digital age. The balance between stringent data protection requirements and effective regulatory enforcement illustrates Germany's proactive stance in addressing the complexities of modern digital governance.

Digital Privacy Laws.

The General Data Protection Regulation (GDPR) serves as the cornerstone of digital privacy protection in Germany, establishing extensive rights for individuals regarding their personal data. Effective since 2018, the GDPR grants rights such as access, rectification, erasure (the "right to be forgotten"), and data portability, enabling individuals to control how their personal information is collected, processed, and shared. The GDPR's consent requirements are stringent, necessitating explicit and informed consent for data processing activities, with a clear right to withdraw consent at any time. Organizations that fail to comply with GDPR requirements face severe penalties, including fines of up to 20 million euros or 4% of their global annual revenue, whichever is higher. This framework has positioned Germany as a leading advocate for data privacy both within the European Union and globally.

To complement the GDPR, Germany has enacted the Federal Data Protection Act (BDSG), which introduces additional safeguards, particularly concerning employee data. The BDSG sets forth specific requirements for the collection, processing, and storage of employee information, mandating that such data must be collected transparently and only for legitimate purposes. It also requires companies to appoint data protection officers if they process personal data on a large scale, enhancing accountability and compliance. The Federal Commissioner for Data Protection and Freedom of Information (BfDI) is responsible for overseeing GDPR and BDSG compliance, conducting audits, and handling complaints from individuals regarding data protection violations.

Germany's emphasis on privacy extends to telecommunications, with the Telecommunications Act (TKG) and the Telemedia Act (TMG) imposing strict confidentiality and security requirements on service providers. These laws mandate clear disclosures regarding data collection practices and prohibit unauthorized access to communications. Together, these measures reflect Germany's comprehensive approach to protecting digital privacy in an increasingly interconnected world.

Online Consumer Protection Laws.

Germany's approach to online consumer protection is characterized by a blend of national laws and EU directives that ensure transparency, fairness, and security in digital transactions. The Civil Code (Bürgerliches Gesetzbuch, BGB) plays a central role in this framework, providing extensive protections against unfair contractual terms and misleading advertising. Under the BGB, consumers have the right to withdraw from online contracts within 14 days without penalty, and sellers are required to provide clear information about product prices, terms of service, and return policies. These provisions are particularly relevant in the context of e-commerce, where complex terms and conditions can often obscure consumers' rights.

The Telemedia Act (TMG) further enhances online consumer protection by requiring online service providers to inform users transparently about data collection practices, cookie usage, and privacy policies. Service providers must also implement appropriate security measures to protect personal data from unauthorized access and breaches. The Federal Office of Justice (BfJ) is responsible for enforcing these regulations, ensuring that online businesses adhere to transparency and security standards.

In addition to national laws, Germany enforces several key EU directives aimed at protecting consumers in digital markets. The Consumer Rights Directive and the E-Commerce Directive mandate clear information on products, services, and consumer rights during online transactions. These directives also ensure secure payment methods and provide consumers with a statutory right of withdrawal from online contracts. The Price Indication Ordinance (PAngV) complements these measures by requiring sellers to display total prices, including taxes and additional costs, ensuring that consumers are not misled by hidden charges.

Tech-Facilitated Crime Laws.

Germany has developed a comprehensive legal framework to combat tech-facilitated crime, combining national laws with EU directives to address threats such as hacking, online fraud, and cyber espionage. The Criminal Code (Strafgesetzbuch, StGB) includes specific provisions for unauthorized access to computer systems (Section 202a), data tampering (Section 303a), and computer fraud (Section 263a). Penalties for these offenses range from fines to imprisonment, depending on the severity and impact of the crime. The Federal Criminal Police Office (Bundeskriminalamt, BKA) leads investigations into serious cybercrimes, collaborating with international partners to address cross-border threats.

A key component of Germany's response to tech-facilitated crime is the Network Enforcement Act (NetzDG), which was enacted in 2017 to combat hate speech, fake news, and extremist content on social media platforms. The NetzDG requires platforms with over two million users to remove clearly illegal content within 24 hours of notification or face fines of up to 50 million euros. The law also mandates transparency reports from platforms, detailing the number of complaints received and actions taken. While the NetzDG has been praised for addressing harmful online content, it has also faced criticism for potentially stifling free speech due to its stringent compliance requirements.

Germany's commitment to cybersecurity is further reinforced by the NIS Directive (Directive on Security of Network and Information Systems), which mandates that operators of essential services and digital service providers implement robust security measures and report cybersecurity incidents to the Federal Office for Information Security (BSI). The BSI plays a critical role in coordinating national cybersecurity efforts, providing guidance to businesses on best practices and managing the national CERT (Computer Emergency Response Team) to respond to cyber incidents swiftly.

Germany's international collaboration on cybercrime is exemplified by its participation in the Budapest Convention on Cybercrime, the first international treaty seeking to harmonize cybercrime laws and facilitate cooperation between countries. The Convention requires member states to criminalize activities such as hacking, computer-related fraud, and child exploitation, ensuring a coordinated response to transnational cyber threats.

Challenges and Future Directions.

Despite its comprehensive legal framework, Germany faces ongoing challenges in balancing privacy, security, and innovation. The stringent requirements of the GDPR and BDSG, while providing robust privacy protections, impose significant compliance burdens on small and medium-sized enterprises (SMEs). Additionally, debates continue around the scope and application of the NetzDG, particularly regarding its impact on freedom of expression and its compatibility with broader EU regulations on digital services.

Looking forward, Germany is focusing on expanding its legal framework to address emerging challenges such as artificial intelligence, digital sovereignty, and data governance. Proposals under consideration include a national AI strategy that emphasizes ethical guidelines for algorithmic decision-making and enhanced protections against AI-driven discrimination. Additionally, discussions are ongoing about the regulation of cloud services and the creation of a national cloud infrastructure to reduce dependence on foreign providers.

Overall, Germany's approach to digital privacy, consumer protection, and tech-facilitated crime reflects a balance between protecting individual rights and enforcing stringent regulations on technology companies. By integrating both national and EU laws, Germany maintains a comprehensive and secure digital legal environment that serves as a model for other countries navigating the complexities of the digital age.

3.6.5 Vietnam

Vietnam has developed a comprehensive legal framework for managing digital privacy, online consumer protection, and tech-facilitated crime, reflecting its centralized governance model and prioritization of national security. This framework is characterized by stringent data localization requirements, extensive government control over online content, and a proactive approach to regulating the rapidly growing digital economy. Vietnam's legal system, influenced by its one-party structure and socialist principles, places a strong emphasis on state sovereignty and public order, often at the expense of individual privacy rights and freedoms.

Digital Privacy Laws.

Vietnam's approach to digital privacy is primarily governed by the Cybersecurity Law (2019), which establishes stringent requirements for data localization and online content management. The law mandates that foreign technology companies operating in Vietnam, such as Facebook, Google, and Apple, must store data concerning Vietnamese users on local servers and establish representative offices in the country. The data localization requirement applies to a broad range of information, including personal data, financial information, and any data deemed important to national security. This aspect of the law has been controversial, with critics arguing that it creates significant compliance costs for foreign companies and raises concerns about surveillance and censorship.

The Cybersecurity Law also grants the Vietnamese government extensive powers to monitor, censor, and block online content that is considered threatening to national security, social order, or the authority of the Communist Party. Internet service providers (ISPs) and social media platforms are required to remove "anti-state" content within 24 hours of receiving a government request or face substantial fines and potential suspension of their services. The law's broad definitions of "national security" and "anti-state" content have raised significant concerns regarding freedom of expression and privacy, with human rights organizations criticizing the law for facilitating government censorship and surveillance.

Complementing the Cybersecurity Law, the Law on Cyber Information Security regulates data collection practices and prohibits unauthorized access to information systems. Enacted in 2015, this law mandates that organizations collecting personal data must obtain user consent, inform individuals about the purpose of data collection, and implement appropriate security measures to prevent unauthorized access or disclosure. It also prohibits the use of malware, spyware, and other malicious software to collect information without user consent. The law's provisions apply broadly to both domestic and international companies operating in Vietnam, underscoring the government's emphasis on data sovereignty.

The enforcement of these privacy laws is overseen by the Ministry of Public Security (MPS), which has extensive authority to conduct inspections, issue fines, and prosecute violations. The MPS also collaborates with the Ministry of Information and Communications (MIC) to monitor compliance with content regulation requirements, further consolidating the state's control over the digital landscape.

Online Consumer Protection Laws.

Vietnam's online consumer protection framework is governed by the Law on Consumer Protection (2010), which establishes a comprehensive set of rights for consumers engaging in e-commerce and other digital transactions. This law mandates that online sellers provide accurate and complete information about products and services, including prices, payment terms, and return policies. Sellers are also required to disclose their business registration information and ensure that consumers can access customer support services to resolve disputes efficiently.

The Law on Consumer Protection grants consumers the right to refunds, returns, and compensation for defective or misrepresented products, which has been instrumental in building consumer trust in Vietnam's rapidly expanding e-commerce sector. Platforms like Shopee, Lazada, and Tiki are required to comply with these standards, and violations can result in substantial fines, suspension of business licenses, or criminal prosecution in severe cases.

To enhance consumer protection in digital markets, the E-Commerce Law (2013) imposes additional requirements on online platforms to verify the authenticity of products, prevent counterfeit sales, and ensure secure payment methods. It also mandates that online businesses adopt measures to safeguard personal data collected during transactions, including encryption and secure authentication methods. The enforcement of these consumer protection laws is managed by the Vietnam Competition and Consumer Authority (VCCA), which conducts investigations, resolves consumer complaints, and coordinates with other regulatory bodies to ensure compliance.

Vietnam's online consumer protection laws reflect a proactive approach to regulating e-commerce, balancing the need to protect consumers with the goal of fostering a secure and trustworthy digital marketplace. The rapid growth of e-commerce in Vietnam, driven by increasing internet penetration and a young, tech-savvy population, has made these regulations particularly significant.

Tech-Facilitated Crime Laws.

Vietnam has developed a comprehensive legal framework to combat tech-facilitated crime, focusing on both national security and public safety. The Penal Code (revised in 2017) includes detailed provisions addressing cybercrimes such as hacking, online fraud, identity theft, and the dissemination of false information. Specifically, the Penal Code criminalizes unauthorized access to computer networks, distribution of malware, phishing, and financial fraud conducted through digital means. Penalties for these offenses range from fines and asset forfeiture to imprisonment, depending on the severity of the crime and its impact on public order and national security.

The Cybersecurity Law (2019) expands on these provisions by authorizing the Ministry of Public Security (MPS) to take direct action against cyber threats, including shutting down websites, blocking access to specific content, and conducting surveillance on suspected individuals or organizations. The MPS operates a dedicated Department of Cybersecurity and High-Tech Crime Prevention, which focuses on identifying and dismantling criminal networks operating online, particularly those involved in financial fraud, child exploitation, and anti-state activities.

Vietnam's focus on national security is also evident in its use of surveillance technologies and extensive monitoring of social media platforms for content deemed to threaten political stability. The government's ability to control internet infrastructure through state-owned ISPs facilitates rapid responses to perceived threats, including blocking access to international news websites and social media platforms during periods of political unrest. While these measures have been effective in controlling online crime, they have also raised concerns about privacy rights and freedom of expression.

Challenges and Future Directions.

Despite its comprehensive legal framework, Vietnam faces significant challenges in balancing security and privacy. The broad scope of the Cybersecurity Law's provisions, coupled with the lack of independent judicial oversight, has led to accusations of state censorship and suppression of dissent. The data localization requirements have also raised concerns among foreign businesses about compliance costs and potential conflicts with international trade agreements, including the Comprehensive and Progressive Agreement for Trans-Pacific Partnership (CPTPP), which Vietnam has ratified.

Looking forward, Vietnam is considering further updates to its legal framework to address emerging challenges, such as the regulation of artificial intelligence, financial technology (fintech), and cross-border data transfers. Proposals include introducing a comprehensive data protection law that aligns more closely with international standards, enhancing transparency in data processing practices, and creating clearer mechanisms for data breach reporting and response.

Overall, Vietnam's legal framework for digital privacy, online consumer protection, and tech-facilitated crime reflects a state-centric approach that prioritizes national security and centralized control over the digital environment. While these measures have been effective in addressing immediate security concerns, ongoing reforms will be crucial for balancing state control with the need for greater transparency, privacy protections, and alignment with international standards.

3.6.6 France

France has established a comprehensive and robust legal framework to address digital privacy, online consumer protection, and tech-facilitated crime, reflecting its commitment to protecting individual rights and ensuring a transparent digital environment. As a member of the European Union, France integrates national laws with EU directives and regulations, creating a cohesive approach to digital governance. France's legal system, based on civil law traditions, emphasizes codified statutes, judicial oversight, and a proactive stance on emerging digital challenges, such as misinformation, data privacy, and cybersecurity.

Digital Privacy Laws.

France's approach to digital privacy is anchored by the General Data Protection Regulation (GDPR), which has been in effect since 2018 and serves as the cornerstone of data protection across the European Union. The GDPR establishes comprehensive rights for individuals regarding their personal data, including the right to access, rectification, erasure (the "right to be forgotten"), and data portability. It imposes strict consent requirements for data collection and processing, with substantial fines for non-compliance, up to 20 million euros or 4% of global annual revenue, whichever is higher. France's enforcement of the GDPR is particularly rigorous, with the Commission Nationale de l'Informatique et des Libertés (CNIL), the French Data Protection Authority, leading numerous high-profile investigations and imposing significant fines on major tech companies for privacy violations.

In addition to the GDPR, France has enacted the French Data Protection Act (Loi Informatique et Libertés), which supplements EU regulations by providing additional safeguards for biometric and genetic data. This Act mandates that the collection and processing of biometric data, such as facial recognition and fingerprints, require explicit consent and must adhere to strict security standards. It also grants the CNIL enhanced enforcement powers, including the ability to conduct on-site inspections, issue binding orders, and levy fines for breaches. The French Data Protection Act demonstrates France's commitment to maintaining high privacy standards while addressing the unique challenges posed by advanced biometric technologies.

The Digital Republic Law (Loi pour une République numérique), enacted in 2016, further strengthens France's digital privacy framework by promoting open data, transparency, and individual rights. The law mandates that public data must be freely accessible in open formats, enhancing transparency in public administration. It also introduces new rights for internet users, such as the right to data portability and the right to control their digital identity, including the ability to request the deletion of online accounts. The Digital Republic Law's emphasis on open data and transparency reflects a balanced approach to privacy that supports both innovation and individual rights.

Online Consumer Protection Laws.

France has a well-established legal framework for online consumer protection, characterized by a combination of national laws and EU directives that safeguard consumers' rights in digital transactions. The Hammon Law (Loi Hamon), enacted in 2014, is a key component of this framework, providing clear rights for online shoppers, including extended refund periods, transparent pricing, and protections against misleading advertising. Under the Hammon Law, consumers have the right to withdraw from online contracts within 14 days without penalty and are entitled to full refunds for returned products. Additionally, online retailers are required to disclose all costs associated with purchases, including delivery fees and potential surcharges, ensuring that consumers are fully informed before making a transaction.

The Hammon Law also strengthens protections against misleading advertising by requiring that promotional offers, discounts, and comparative advertisements must be clearly substantiated and not deceptive. The law empowers the Directorate General for Competition, Consumer Affairs and Fraud Control (DGCCRF) to investigate violations and impose fines, conduct inspections, and order corrective actions. This proactive enforcement approach has been instrumental in maintaining consumer trust in France's rapidly expanding e-commerce market.

In addition to the Hammon Law, France enforces several EU directives aimed at protecting consumers online, including the Consumer Rights Directive and the E-Commerce Directive. These directives mandate that online platforms provide clear information about terms of service, secure payment methods, and user-friendly dispute resolution mechanisms. The Price Transparency Law complements these measures by requiring that all prices displayed online include taxes and mandatory fees, preventing deceptive pricing practices. Together, these laws ensure a transparent and fair digital marketplace in France, enhancing consumer confidence and trust in online transactions.

Tech-Facilitated Crime Laws.

France has developed a comprehensive legal framework to combat tech-facilitated crime, addressing a range of threats from hacking and online fraud to misinformation and cyber espionage. The French Penal Code (Code Pénal) includes detailed provisions for cybercrimes, criminalizing unauthorized access to computer systems, data breaches, and the distribution of malware. Penalties for these offenses include fines and imprisonment, with enhanced penalties for crimes targeting critical infrastructure or involving sensitive personal data. The Central Office for the Fight against Crime Linked to Information and Communication Technology (OCLCTIC) leads investigations into cybercrimes, working closely with other European and international law enforcement agencies to address cross-border threats.

In response to the growing threat of misinformation, particularly during election periods, France enacted the Anti-Fake News Law (Loi contre la manipulation de l'information) in 2018. This law targets misinformation by requiring online platforms to remove false content promptly and implement mechanisms to flag and verify information during election campaigns. It also grants judicial authorities the power to order the removal of content deemed to intentionally spread false information that could influence electoral outcomes. Platforms that fail to comply with these requirements face significant fines and potential suspension. While the Anti-Fake News Law has been praised for addressing the rapid spread of misinformation, it has also raised concerns about potential censorship and the balance between content regulation and freedom of expression.

France's cybersecurity framework is further bolstered by the Military Programming Law (Loi de programmation militaire), which mandates that operators of essential services implement stringent cybersecurity measures and report incidents promptly to the National Cybersecurity Agency of France (ANSSI). The ANSSI plays a crucial role in coordinating national cybersecurity efforts, providing guidance on best practices, conducting risk assessments, and managing incident responses.

Challenges and Future Directions.

Despite its comprehensive legal framework, France faces challenges in balancing privacy, security, and freedom of expression, particularly concerning content regulation and data localization requirements. The Anti-Fake News Law, while effective in combating misinformation, has sparked debates about potential overreach and the risk of stifling legitimate political discourse. Additionally, France's proactive enforcement of the GDPR, exemplified by high-profile fines against tech giants, has led to tensions with businesses regarding compliance costs and regulatory predictability.

Looking forward, France is focusing on expanding its legal framework to address emerging challenges such as artificial intelligence, digital sovereignty, and the regulation of cloud services. Proposed regulations include measures to ensure that AI systems adhere to ethical guidelines and do not perpetuate biases or violate privacy rights. Additionally, France is advocating for an EU-wide approach to regulating cloud services, emphasizing data sovereignty and reducing dependence on foreign providers.

Overall, France's approach to digital privacy, online consumer protection, and tech-facilitated crime reflects a balance between protecting individual rights and maintaining a secure and transparent digital environment. By integrating national laws with EU regulations and adopting a proactive stance on enforcement, France has positioned itself as a leader in digital governance, setting high standards for privacy, security, and consumer protection in the European Union.

3.7 Chapter Summary

Understanding the principles of lawmaking, the processes involved in legislation, and the mechanisms of enforcement is essential for effectively addressing the complex and evolving legal challenges posed by cybercrime. As this chapter has demonstrated, laws and legislation form the foundational framework that governs behavior, protects individual rights, and ensures justice in both physical and digital environments. The processes of creating, amending, and enforcing laws are not only fundamental to maintaining public order but are also crucial for adapting legal systems to emerging threats, particularly those associated with advancements in information technology and cybercrime.

The comparative analysis presented in this chapter highlights the diverse approaches that different countries adopt to regulate digital privacy, protect online consumers, and combat tech-facilitated crime. For instance, while countries like Germany and France have established comprehensive legal frameworks aligned with the General Data Protection Regulation (GDPR) to safeguard privacy rights, nations such as China and Vietnam emphasize state control and data localization to maintain national security and social stability. Similarly, the United States' fragmented but robust legal landscape reflects a balance between state-specific privacy regulations and federal initiatives to combat online fraud and unauthorized data access. These variations underscore the influence of political systems, cultural values, and economic priorities on national legal frameworks.

Moreover, the role of international cooperation in combating cross-border cyber threats has become increasingly significant. Legal instruments such as the Budapest Convention on Cybercrime and bilateral agreements for data sharing and mutual legal assistance illustrate the need for harmonized legal standards and collaborative enforcement strategies. However, challenges persist, including jurisdictional conflicts, divergent privacy standards, and the balance between privacy rights and national security imperatives. As cybercriminals continue to exploit gaps in international law, the development of cohesive and enforceable global legal standards remains a critical objective.

The enforcement of laws, as examined across different jurisdictions, reveals a complex interplay between law enforcement agencies, regulatory bodies, and judicial systems. Effective enforcement requires not only comprehensive laws but also adequate resources, specialized expertise, and mechanisms for cross-border collaboration. Countries like Canada and Germany demonstrate the effectiveness of centralized regulatory bodies, such as the Federal Office for Information Security (BSI) and the Royal Canadian Mounted Police (RCMP), in coordinating national cybersecurity efforts. In contrast, the extensive surveillance capabilities of China's Ministry of Public Security (MPS) highlight the challenges of balancing security with individual privacy rights.

This chapter also underscores the importance of legislative adaptability in addressing emerging challenges such as artificial intelligence, blockchain, and data sovereignty. As new technologies reshape the digital landscape, the need for updated legal frameworks that balance innovation with security and privacy becomes more pressing. The ongoing legislative efforts in the European Union to regulate AI ethics and cloud services, as well as the proposed updates to privacy laws in the United States and Canada, indicate a proactive approach to these challenges.

In addition to exploring national and international legal frameworks, the chapter has highlighted the ethical implications of digital governance, particularly concerning content regulation, misinformation, and censorship. The varying approaches to regulating online content, from France's Anti-Fake News Law to Vietnam's stringent censorship measures, raise important questions about the limits of free speech in the digital age. As governments continue to grapple with the dual imperatives of security and freedom, the ethical dimensions of lawmaking and enforcement will require careful consideration.

Looking forward, subsequent chapters will delve deeper into the specific legal frameworks governing cybercrime, examining in detail how various countries address issues such as data breaches, ransomware, intellectual property theft, and the dark web. These chapters will also explore the role of international organizations, such as Interpol and the European Union Agency for Cybersecurity (ENISA), in fostering cooperation and standardization in cyber law. Additionally, the impact of public awareness, corporate compliance programs, and emerging technologies on the efficacy of cyber laws will be analyzed, providing a comprehensive understanding of the multifaceted battle against cybercrime.

By integrating insights from different legal systems and examining both the strengths and limitations of existing frameworks, the forthcoming chapters aim to equip readers with a nuanced understanding of the legal landscape surrounding cybercrime. This knowledge will be crucial for policymakers, law enforcement professionals, and cybersecurity experts seeking to develop effective legal and operational strategies to counter the growing threat of cybercrime in an increasingly interconnected world.

Chapter 4
The Impacts of Cybercrime: From Micro to Macro Levels

This chapter examines the impacts of cybercrime through a wide lens, progressing from micro-level effects on individual victims to macro-level consequences for national security, economic stability, and international relations. Understanding these impacts is essential for criminology, law, computer science, and cybersecurity students seeking to develop effective prevention, mitigation, and response strategies.

4.1 Introduction

Cybercrime has rapidly emerged as one of the most significant threats to individuals, organizations, and nations in the digital age. As our dependence on information technology has grown, so too have the risks posed by malicious actors who exploit vulnerabilities for financial gain, ideological motives, or sheer disruption. The impacts of cybercrime are profound and multifaceted, affecting victims at every level, from individuals who fall prey to identity theft to entire nations grappling with threats to critical infrastructure and national security.

4.2 Micro-Level Impacts: The Individual Victims of Cybercrime

At the micro level, the impacts of cybercrime on individual victims can be profound, affecting their psychological well-being, financial stability, and social reputation. Unlike traditional crimes, which are often constrained by geographical boundaries and physical presence, cybercrimes can reach victims anywhere, at any time, with devastating immediacy and scale. The anonymity afforded to perpetrators and the pervasive nature of digital platforms amplify these impacts, leaving victims feeling

M. K. A. Lukings et al., *Understanding Cybercrime Victim Services*, Progress in IS,
https://doi.org/10.1007/978-3-032-13273-4_4

powerless and exposed. The constant connectivity of modern life further exacerbates these vulnerabilities, making it difficult for victims to escape the reach of cybercriminals or mitigate the harm inflicted.

This section explores the multifaceted effects of cybercrime on individuals, focusing on the psychological distress caused by privacy violations and online harassment, the financial losses resulting from identity theft and fraud, and the long-term reputational damage that can follow from the unauthorized dissemination of personal information. Understanding these impacts is essential for developing effective support systems, legal protections, and preventive measures that address the unique vulnerabilities of individual victims in the digital age.

4.2.1 Psychological Impacts

For individual victims, the psychological impacts of cybercrime can be severe and long-lasting. Victims of identity theft, online harassment, revenge porn, and financial fraud often experience heightened levels of stress, anxiety, and feelings of powerlessness. The sense of violation associated with cybercrimes like doxxing, where an individual's personal information is publicly exposed, can lead to acute psychological distress, social withdrawal, and, in severe cases, post-traumatic stress disorder (PTSD). The anonymity of online attackers exacerbates these impacts, leaving victims with a persistent sense of vulnerability and mistrust of digital platforms.

Hypothetical Example:
Consider a hypothetical case where Emma, a college student, becomes the target of cyberbullying after a former friend creates anonymous social media accounts to spread false rumors and share edited photos of her. Despite reporting the accounts, Emma finds that new ones appear almost immediately, making it impossible to stop the attacks. The relentless harassment leads to severe anxiety, depression, and a withdrawal from both online and offline social interactions. Emma's grades and personal relationships suffer, illustrating the profound psychological toll that sustained cyberbullying can inflict.

Addressing these impacts requires not only robust legal protections but also accessible psychological support services and educational programs aimed at fostering digital resilience. Effective victim support systems should include crisis counseling, mental health services, and specialized helplines that provide practical advice for managing the psychological aftermath of cyber incidents.

4.2.2 Financial Impacts

The financial consequences of cybercrime for individuals can be devastating and, in many cases, far exceed the immediate losses incurred. Identity theft and financial fraud, such as credit card fraud, phishing scams, and unauthorized transactions, often result in substantial economic losses, prolonged disputes with financial institutions, and damaged credit scores. The process of restoring one's financial standing can be protracted and burdensome.

Hypothetical Example:
Imagine a scenario in which James, a freelance graphic designer, falls victim to a phishing scam disguised as a payment request from a trusted client. Unknowingly, he provides his banking information to the attacker, resulting in the withdrawal of $5,000 from his business account. Beyond the immediate financial loss, James spends months disputing the charges, securing loans to cover his business expenses, and repairing his damaged credit score. The financial strain forces him to delay critical software upgrades and marketing efforts, impacting his business's growth and profitability.

The financial impacts are also magnified by the erosion of trust in digital financial systems. Addressing these impacts requires comprehensive financial education, stronger consumer protection laws, and improved access to legal remedies for victims of financial cybercrime.

4.2.3 *Social and Reputational Impacts*

Cybercrime also has significant social and reputational impacts on individuals, often with irreversible consequences. Online defamation, revenge porn, and the unauthorized sharing of private information can irreparably damage personal relationships, professional reputations, and employment prospects. The viral nature of social media amplifies these impacts.

Hypothetical Example:
Consider a hypothetical case involving Sarah, a public relations professional, who becomes the victim of a deepfake video falsely depicting her making derogatory remarks about her employer. The video goes viral, leading to her immediate suspension from her job pending investigation. Despite proving that the video was fabricated, the online backlash and media coverage cause lasting damage to her professional reputation, resulting in lost clients, a tarnished LinkedIn profile, and ongoing difficulties in securing new employment opportunities.

Efforts to restore reputations, such as hiring online reputation management services, can be costly and are not always successful in mitigating the long-term effects. Addressing these impacts requires stronger legal protections, including the right to be forgotten, clearer procedures for content removal, and enhanced regulatory oversight of social media platforms.

4.2.4 *Legal and Procedural Impacts*

In addition to psychological, financial, and reputational impacts, victims of cybercrime often face significant legal and procedural challenges. Navigating the legal system to report cybercrimes, pursue civil remedies, or seek compensation can be a daunting and resource-intensive process.

Hypothetical Example:
Imagine a hypothetical scenario where Michael, a small business owner, discovers that his company's website has been hacked, with customer payment information stolen and sold on the dark web. When he attempts to report the incident, he is directed between local law enforcement, a national cybersecurity agency, and his web hosting provider, each of whom claims limited jurisdiction over the case. The lack of clarity and the complexity of the reporting process leave Michael frustrated and without a clear path to justice, highlighting the procedural hurdles that many victims face.

Addressing these legal and procedural impacts requires harmonization of cybercrime laws across jurisdictions, greater investment in law enforcement training, and simplified legal processes that empower victims to pursue justice more effectively.

4.2.5 *Conclusion*

The micro-level impacts of cybercrime on individuals are profound and multifaceted, extending beyond immediate financial losses to encompass long-term psychological distress, social isolation, and reputational harm. The hypothetical examples presented illustrate the diverse ways in which cybercrime can disrupt lives, erode trust in digital platforms, and create significant barriers to recovery. Understanding these impacts is essential for developing effective legal frameworks, support systems, and educational programs aimed at empowering victims and preventing further harm. As cyber threats continue to evolve, a victim-centered approach to cybersecurity and law enforcement will be crucial for addressing the unique vulnerabilities of individuals in the digital age.

4.3 Meso-Level Impacts: Organizations and Businesses

At the meso level, the impacts of cybercrime on organizations and businesses are both severe and multifaceted, encompassing financial losses, operational disruptions, reputational damage, and strategic vulnerabilities. As businesses increasingly rely on digital infrastructure to manage operations, store sensitive information, and engage with customers, they become prime targets for cybercriminals seeking financial gain, competitive intelligence, or political leverage. The rising sophistication of cyber threats, ranging from ransomware and phishing to cyber espionage, poses a significant challenge to organizational security and risk management.

The consequences of cybercrime for organizations extend beyond immediate financial losses. Long-term reputational damage, regulatory penalties, and strategic disadvantages can undermine an organization's competitiveness and market position. Additionally, the operational disruptions caused by ransomware attacks and data breaches can halt production, disrupt supply chains, and erode customer trust. Effective responses to these threats require comprehensive cybersecurity strategies that integrate prevention, detection, response, and recovery measures.

This section examines the financial and operational impacts of cybercrime, focusing on the direct costs of data breaches and business disruptions, as well as the indirect costs associated with recovery efforts and regulatory compliance. It also explores the reputational and compliance impacts of cyber incidents, highlighting how failures in data security can erode customer trust and attract regulatory penalties. Finally, the section analyzes the strategic and competitive consequences of cyber espionage, emphasizing the long-term risks to innovation, market positioning, and investment capacity. Understanding these meso-level impacts is crucial for organizations to develop comprehensive cybersecurity strategies that protect not only their assets but also their reputations and competitive standing in an increasingly digital economy.

4.3.1 Financial and Operational Impacts

For organizations and businesses, the financial and operational impacts of cybercrime are substantial. Data breaches, ransomware attacks, and business email compromise (BEC) schemes can result in direct financial losses, disruption of business operations, and significant recovery costs. According to studies, the average cost of a data breach can exceed millions of dollars when accounting for legal fees, compensation to affected customers, forensic investigations, and system upgrades.

Operational disruptions can be particularly severe for businesses dependent on real-time data and digital infrastructure. For instance, ransomware attacks that encrypt critical databases can halt production lines, disrupt supply chains, and prevent businesses from fulfilling contractual obligations, resulting in lost revenue and legal liabilities.

Hypothetical Example:
Imagine a hypothetical scenario in which BrightSpark Electronics, a mid-sized manufacturer of smart home devices, becomes the target of a ransomware attack. The attackers encrypt the company's production databases and demand a ransom of $500,000 in cryptocurrency. Refusing to pay, BrightSpark spends nearly $2 million on forensic investigations, system upgrades, and overtime for IT staff to restore operations. During the three-week recovery period, the company fails to meet contractual

obligations to major retailers, resulting in additional financial penalties and strained business relationships. The total financial impact, including lost revenue, operational costs, and reputational damage, exceeds $5 million.

This example illustrates how the financial and operational impacts of cybercrime can extend far beyond the initial ransom demand, affecting every aspect of a business's operations and profitability.

4.3.2 Reputational and Compliance Impacts

The reputational damage following a cyber incident can be as harmful as the financial impacts. Customers are increasingly sensitive to data privacy and security practices, and a poorly handled breach can lead to lasting damage to brand trust and customer loyalty. Organizations that fail to notify customers promptly or demonstrate transparency in their response often face consumer backlash, negative media coverage, and declining market share.

Compliance impacts are also significant, particularly under regulatory frameworks like the General Data Protection Regulation (GDPR) and the California Consumer Privacy Act (CCPA), which mandate stringent data protection measures and substantial penalties for non-compliance. Organizations that fail to meet these standards not only face regulatory fines but also risk being barred from doing business in critical markets.

Hypothetical Example:
Consider a hypothetical case where MediSure Health, a private healthcare provider, suffers a data breach exposing the medical records of 500,000 patients. The breach is traced back to a third-party vendor's insecure file-sharing system. Despite being aware of the incident, MediSure delays notifying affected patients for nearly a month. When the breach is finally disclosed, public outrage escalates, leading to a significant loss of patient trust and a 20% drop in new patient registrations over the following six months. Regulatory bodies impose fines totaling $3 million for non-compliance with GDPR's breach notification requirements, further compounding the financial and reputational damage.

This example demonstrates how delayed responses and non-compliance can transform a cyber incident into a full-blown crisis with lasting reputational and financial impacts.

4.3.3 Strategic and Competitive Impacts

Cyber espionage targeting trade secrets and intellectual property can have profound strategic and competitive impacts. Theft of proprietary information such as product designs, manufacturing processes, or strategic plans can erode competitive advantages, result in lost market opportunities, and undermine innovation. In sectors such as pharmaceuticals, aerospace, and technology, the loss of sensitive R&D information can set back product development by years.

Additionally, the threat of cyberattacks has forced organizations to divert substantial resources to cybersecurity measures, impacting their ability to invest in other strategic priorities. This growing expenditure on cybersecurity has become a critical aspect of business strategy and risk management.

Hypothetical Example:
Imagine a hypothetical scenario where Aurora Pharmaceuticals, a biotech company, is developing a breakthrough cancer treatment. A state-sponsored hacking group infiltrates the company's network, stealing proprietary research data and clinical trial results. Six months later, a foreign competitor announces a remarkably similar drug, undercutting Aurora's market advantage. The loss of intellectual property forces Aurora to delay its product launch and absorb significant legal and R&D costs to revise its formulations and strengthen cybersecurity defenses. Analysts estimate that the breach cost the company over $300 million in lost market opportunities and competitive advantage.

This example highlights how cyber espionage can directly impact an organization's strategic positioning, eroding competitive advantages and diminishing returns on innovation.

4.3.4 Legal and Procedural Impacts

In addition to financial, reputational, and strategic impacts, businesses often face significant legal and procedural challenges following a cyber incident. The complexity of compliance with data protection regulations, cross-border legal obligations, and the potential for class-action lawsuits can create substantial legal liabilities.

Hypothetical Example:
Consider a hypothetical case where GlobalTrans Logistics, an international shipping company, experiences a cyberattack that compromises customer data across three continents. The attack triggers legal obligations under GDPR in Europe, CCPA in California, and multiple other data protection laws worldwide. Within weeks, several class-action lawsuits are filed by affected customers seeking compensation for data misuse. The complexity of coordinating legal responses across jurisdictions, coupled with the threat of multi-million-dollar fines, forces GlobalTrans to allocate nearly $10 million to legal defenses and regulatory compliance measures.

This example illustrates the extensive legal and procedural challenges that can arise from cross-border data breaches, highlighting the importance of robust legal and compliance strategies.

4.3.5 *Conclusion*

The meso-level impacts of cybercrime on organizations and businesses are profound, encompassing financial losses, operational disruptions, reputational damage, and strategic disadvantages. The hypothetical examples presented illustrate the diverse ways in which cybercrime can threaten business continuity, erode trust, and compromise competitive positioning. Understanding these impacts is essential for organizations seeking to develop comprehensive cybersecurity strategies that integrate prevention, detection, and response capabilities. As cyber threats continue to evolve, a proactive and integrated approach to cybersecurity will be crucial for protecting not only organizational assets but also long-term growth and innovation.

4.4 Macro-Level Impacts: National and International Dimensions

At the macro level, the impacts of cybercrime extend far beyond individual victims and organizations, posing significant threats to national security, economic stability, and international relations. As cybercriminals and state-sponsored actors exploit the interconnectedness of digital infrastructure, the consequences of their actions can ripple across borders, disrupting critical services, undermining trust in financial systems, and escalating geopolitical tensions. The scale, sophistication, and transnational nature of these threats necessitate comprehensive national cybersecurity strategies, robust international cooperation, and the development of universally accepted norms to govern state conduct in cyberspace.

The economic impacts of cybercrime are measured not only in direct financial losses but also in reduced productivity, diminished investor confidence, and escalating costs of cybersecurity measures. At the national security level, cyberattacks targeting critical infrastructure, military systems, and electoral processes pose direct threats to sovereignty and public safety. The geopolitical ramifications of cybercrime further complicate international relations, as accusations of state-sponsored attacks and espionage lead to rising tensions, sanctions, and retaliatory measures.

This section explores the profound economic impacts of cybercrime, including the direct financial losses, productivity declines, and escalating costs of cybersecurity measures required to safeguard national infrastructures. It also examines the national security implications of cyber threats, highlighting how state-sponsored attacks on critical infrastructure, military systems, and democratic processes pose direct risks to sovereignty and public safety. Finally, the section analyzes the geopolitical and international relations impacts of cybercrime, focusing on the challenges of attributing state-sponsored attacks, the role of international legal frameworks, and the diplomatic tensions arising from accusations of cyber espionage and interference. Understanding these macro-level impacts is essential for developing effective policies and cooperative strategies to combat cybercrime on a global scale.

4.4.1 *Economic Impacts*

At the macro level, the economic impacts of cybercrime are profound. The global cost of cybercrime is estimated to exceed trillions of dollars annually, encompassing direct losses, productivity declines, and escalating costs related to securing networks and systems. Cyberattacks on critical infrastructure, such as energy grids, financial markets, and healthcare systems, pose systemic risks that can destabilize entire economies. Additionally, cybercrime undermines trust in digital markets, deterring investments and innovation. Governments must allocate significant resources to cybersecurity initiatives, diverting funding from other public services such as healthcare and education.

Hypothetical Example:
Imagine a hypothetical scenario where a major cyberattack targets the financial sector of Nordica, a fictional European country heavily reliant on digital banking systems. A coordinated ransomware attack infects the networks of three leading banks, encrypting transaction data and rendering ATMs, online banking, and payment systems inoperable for five days. The attack causes panic among citizens, leading to a run on cash and temporary closures of businesses. The estimated economic impact, including the cost of recovery, lost business revenues, and damage to consumer confidence, exceeds $2 billion. The government is forced to redirect funds from healthcare and infrastructure projects to bolster cybersecurity defenses and restore public confidence in the financial system.

This example illustrates how cyberattacks targeting critical financial infrastructure can have far-reaching economic impacts, destabilizing entire sectors and necessitating costly government interventions.

4.4.2 *National Security Impacts*

Cybercrime has increasingly blurred the line between criminal and national security threats. State-sponsored cyberattacks targeting critical infrastructure, military systems, and election processes pose direct threats to national sovereignty and public safety. Incidents such as the **Stuxnet attack** on Iran's nuclear facilities and the use of disinformation campaigns to influence democratic elections illustrate the evolving nature of cyber threats. The militarization of cyberspace and the potential for cyber warfare necessitate comprehensive national cybersecurity strategies, international cooperation, and legal frameworks capable of addressing both peacetime and wartime cyber activities.

Hypothetical Example:
Consider a hypothetical case in which Arctonia, a fictional country, experiences a cyberattack on its national power grid, believed to be the work of a state-sponsored hacking group. The attack leads to widespread blackouts across major

cities, disrupting transportation, healthcare services, and communications for 48 h. Hospitals are forced to operate on emergency generators, and train services are suspended, causing chaos and endangering public safety. In the aftermath, Arctonia's intelligence agencies attribute the attack to a foreign government, escalating military tensions and prompting the government to invoke its mutual defense agreements with allied nations.

This example demonstrates how cyberattacks on critical infrastructure can escalate from criminal acts to national security crises, compelling states to respond with both defensive and offensive cyber capabilities.

4.4.3 International Relations and Geopolitical Impacts

The international nature of cybercrime complicates diplomatic relations and raises significant geopolitical challenges. Accusations of state-sponsored cyberattacks have led to escalating tensions, economic sanctions, and retaliatory measures between major powers. The absence of universally accepted norms and regulations governing state conduct in cyberspace further exacerbates these tensions. Efforts to develop international legal frameworks, such as the Budapest Convention on Cybercrime and United Nations initiatives, reflect the growing recognition of the need for global cooperation. However, divergent national interests, concerns over sovereignty, and differing views on internet governance remain significant obstacles.

Hypothetical Example:
Imagine a hypothetical scenario where Vega, a fictional country, accuses a rival state of orchestrating a series of cyberattacks targeting its election infrastructure just weeks before a national vote. The attacks disrupt voter registration databases and spread disinformation campaigns aimed at discrediting candidates. In response, Vega imposes economic sanctions on the rival state and seeks support for a formal condemnation at the United Nations Security Council. The rival state denies the accusations, escalating diplomatic tensions and leading to a series of retaliatory cyber operations targeting Vega's defense and economic sectors.

This example highlights how cybercrime can rapidly escalate into a geopolitical crisis, straining diplomatic relations and complicating efforts to establish international norms and rules of engagement in cyberspace.

4.4.4 Legal and Procedural Impacts

The legal and procedural challenges of addressing cybercrime at the macro level are significant. The lack of harmonized international laws and the challenges of attributing cyberattacks to specific state or non-state actors complicate efforts to hold perpetrators accountable. The complexity of mutual legal assistance treaties

(MLATs) and the absence of a universally binding international treaty on cybercrime hinder timely cooperation between nations.

Hypothetical Example:
Consider a hypothetical case in which Oceania, a fictional island nation, suffers a major data breach compromising the personal information of millions of citizens. The attack is traced to servers located in multiple countries, each with different data protection laws and levels of cooperation with international investigations. Oceania's law enforcement agencies face months of bureaucratic delays in securing mutual legal assistance agreements, slowing the investigation and allowing the attackers to erase traces and move funds through offshore accounts. The lack of streamlined international legal frameworks prevents timely justice and exposes the gaps in current international cybercrime laws.

This example illustrates the urgent need for harmonized international legal frameworks to facilitate timely investigations and prosecutions of transnational cybercrimes.

4.4.5 Conclusion

The macro-level impacts of cybercrime are profound and complex, encompassing economic instability, threats to national security, and escalating geopolitical tensions. The hypothetical examples presented illustrate how cybercrime can destabilize financial systems, compromise critical infrastructure, and strain diplomatic relations between nations. Addressing these challenges requires comprehensive national cybersecurity strategies, robust international cooperation, and the development of universally accepted norms to govern state conduct in cyberspace. As cyber threats continue to evolve, a coordinated and multifaceted approach will be essential for safeguarding national interests and maintaining international peace and security.

4.5 Why Cybercrime Impacts Differ from Traditional Crime Impacts

The impacts of cybercrime differ significantly from those of traditional crime due to the unique characteristics of the digital environment. Unlike traditional crimes, which are typically confined by geographical boundaries and often target specific victims directly, cybercrimes can span multiple jurisdictions, affect vast numbers of victims simultaneously, and leverage anonymity and automation to maximize their impact. The following are key reasons why the impacts of cybercrime are distinct from those associated with non-tech-enabled crimes:

4.5.1 Scale and Reach

One of the most profound differences between cybercrime and traditional crime is the scale at which cybercrimes can occur. Cybercriminals can target thousands or even millions of victims simultaneously with relative ease. For example, a single phishing campaign can distribute fraudulent emails to millions of recipients within minutes, and a data breach can expose the personal information of millions of individuals in a single incident. In contrast, traditional crimes such as burglary or fraud typically target individuals or small groups directly and are limited by physical and logistical constraints.

This vast reach amplifies the financial, psychological, and societal impacts of cybercrime exponentially. The ability to automate attacks through botnets, malware, and ransomware allows cybercriminals to exploit vulnerabilities on a global scale, maximizing profits with minimal risk of detection or prosecution. The global reach of cybercrime also complicates law enforcement efforts, requiring extensive cross-border cooperation, which is often hindered by jurisdictional conflicts and differing legal standards.

4.5.2 Anonymity and Attribution Challenges

Cybercrime's digital nature provides perpetrators with a level of anonymity that is rarely achievable in traditional crimes. Techniques such as encryption, VPNs (Virtual Private Networks), the dark web, and cryptocurrency transactions obscure the identities of cybercriminals and complicate efforts to trace attacks back to their origin. This anonymity not only emboldens perpetrators by reducing the perceived risk of capture but also complicates efforts to deter and prosecute cybercrimes effectively.

In traditional crimes, physical evidence such as fingerprints, surveillance footage, and eyewitness testimonies play a crucial role in identifying and prosecuting offenders. In contrast, the digital evidence required to attribute cybercrimes often involves complex technical analyses of IP addresses, server logs, and network traffic, which can be easily obfuscated. The attribution problem becomes even more challenging when state-sponsored actors engage in sophisticated cyber espionage campaigns designed to mislead investigators through techniques like false-flag operations and proxy attacks.

The lack of reliable attribution mechanisms undermines deterrence, as cybercriminals can operate with relative impunity. For state-sponsored cyberattacks, the difficulty of attribution complicates diplomatic and military responses, raising the risk of miscalculation and escalation in international relations.

4.5.3 Speed and Automation

The speed at which cybercrimes occur distinguishes them significantly from traditional crimes. Automated tools and scripts enable cybercriminals to conduct attacks at a pace that outstrips the capacity of traditional law enforcement responses. For instance, ransomware attacks can encrypt an organization's entire database within minutes, demanding a ransom payment under tight deadlines. Similarly, denial-of-service (DoS) attacks can cripple websites and online services in a matter of seconds, causing immediate and widespread disruption.

In traditional crimes, law enforcement often has the opportunity to intervene during the commission of a crime or in its immediate aftermath. However, the rapid execution and global nature of cybercrimes mean that by the time law enforcement becomes aware of an attack, the damage is often already done, and the perpetrators may have erased digital footprints and moved on.

Moreover, the increasing use of artificial intelligence (AI) and machine learning by cybercriminals has further accelerated the speed of attacks, enabling more sophisticated and targeted campaigns. For example, AI-driven phishing schemes can analyze social media profiles to craft personalized messages that increase the likelihood of success. The automation of cybercrime not only enhances its efficiency but also lowers the entry barriers for perpetrators, enabling even less technically skilled individuals to launch effective attacks using ready-made tools available on the dark web.

4.5.4 Complexity and the Interconnectedness of Systems

The complexity of modern information systems and the interconnectedness of digital infrastructure create unique vulnerabilities that cybercriminals can exploit. Unlike traditional crimes, which often involve discrete incidents with isolated impacts, cybercrimes can trigger cascading effects that impact entire networks, industries, or national infrastructures. For instance, attacks on critical infrastructure such as power grids, water treatment facilities, or financial systems can have widespread and systemic consequences that go far beyond the immediate financial losses.

This interconnectedness means that vulnerabilities in one organization's systems can be exploited to gain access to multiple networks, amplifying the impact of an attack. The 2017 NotPetya attack demonstrated this interconnected vulnerability by using compromised software updates to spread malware globally, causing billions of dollars in damage to multinational corporations, shipping companies, and government agencies.

The complexity of cybercrime is also evident in hybrid attacks that combine elements of financial crime, espionage, and sabotage, often involving multiple stages and tactics. For instance, advanced persistent threats (APTs) involve long-term, stealthy intrusions designed to exfiltrate sensitive information without detection. The sophistication and layered nature of these attacks make them challenging to detect and mitigate, requiring advanced cybersecurity measures and coordinated responses.

4.5.5 Psychological Impacts and Trust Erosion

While traditional crimes can cause psychological distress, the psychological impacts of cybercrime are distinct in their scope and nature. Victims of cyberstalking, revenge porn, and doxxing, for instance, often experience a profound and pervasive sense of violation due to the public and permanent nature of online content. The fact that such content can be shared, archived, and resurfaced indefinitely exacerbates feelings of helplessness and fear. In contrast, traditional crimes are often temporally and geographically confined, allowing victims a clearer path to recovery.

The erosion of trust is another significant impact of cybercrime that differs from traditional crime. High-profile data breaches and financial fraud undermine public confidence in digital platforms, online banking, and e-commerce, impeding the adoption of new technologies and hindering the growth of the digital economy. For organizations, recovering consumer trust following a cyber incident can be a long and costly process, involving extensive public relations efforts, enhanced security measures, and compliance with regulatory requirements.

On a macro level, cyber espionage and election interference have eroded trust in democratic institutions and electoral processes, contributing to political polarization and social fragmentation. The use of deepfakes, disinformation campaigns, and bot-driven social media manipulation has further compounded these impacts by blurring the lines between reality and misinformation, making it increasingly difficult for the public to trust digital content.

4.5.6 Jurisdictional Challenges and Legal Complexity

Traditional crimes are generally confined to specific jurisdictions, allowing law enforcement agencies to investigate, prosecute, and adjudicate cases within clear legal frameworks. In contrast, the transnational nature of cybercrime creates significant jurisdictional challenges, complicating law enforcement efforts and international cooperation. Cybercriminals can operate from countries with weak legal frameworks or from jurisdictions that lack extradition treaties with victims' countries, effectively evading prosecution.

The complexity of applicable laws across different jurisdictions further exacerbates these challenges. While international frameworks like the Budapest Convention on Cybercrime provide a basis for cooperation, the absence of universally accepted norms and the divergence between national legal systems complicate the enforcement of cybercrime laws. Moreover, conflicts between privacy regulations, such as the General Data Protection Regulation (GDPR) in the European Union and surveillance laws in other jurisdictions, add layers of legal complexity that do not typically arise in traditional crime.

4.6 Summary

The impacts of cybercrime differ fundamentally from those of traditional crimes due to the scale, speed, anonymity, and transnational nature of digital threats. Understanding these distinctions is essential for developing effective legal, technical, and policy responses to mitigate the growing risks posed by cybercrime. The next chapter will explore the legal frameworks and international cooperation mechanisms designed to address these unique challenges, examining their effectiveness and limitations in combating cyber threats in an interconnected world.

4.7 Chapter Summary

The impacts of cybercrime extend far beyond individual victims, permeating organizational structures, national economies, and international relations. As this chapter has illustrated, cybercrime poses complex challenges at every level, from the psychological and financial distress suffered by individual victims to the strategic and geopolitical threats faced by nation-states. The multi-level analysis presented here underscores the necessity of adopting a comprehensive approach to cybercrime that addresses its wide-ranging impacts through targeted prevention, mitigation, and response strategies.

At the micro level, individuals are increasingly vulnerable to identity theft, online harassment, and financial fraud, which not only cause immediate economic losses but also result in profound psychological and social repercussions. The erosion of trust in digital platforms further complicates the path to recovery for victims, highlighting the need for stronger legal protections, support services, and public awareness initiatives to enhance digital literacy and resilience.

At the meso level, organizations and businesses face escalating risks from data breaches, ransomware, and cyber espionage, which threaten financial stability, operational continuity, and reputational integrity. Compliance with regulatory frameworks such as the General Data Protection Regulation (GDPR) and the California Consumer Privacy Act (CCPA) has become not just a legal obligation but a strategic imperative. The rising costs associated with cybersecurity investments and breach responses underscore the importance of integrating cybersecurity into core business strategies and risk management practices.

At the macro level, the economic and national security implications of cybercrime are profound. The ability of state and non-state actors to target critical infrastructure, manipulate financial systems, and conduct disinformation campaigns poses significant risks to national sovereignty and international stability. The transnational nature of cyber threats demands enhanced international cooperation, harmonized legal frameworks, and the development of universally accepted norms of state behavior in cyberspace.

The unique characteristics of cybercrime, including its scale, speed, anonymity, and cross-border nature, distinguish it fundamentally from traditional crimes, necessitating specialized legal, technical, and policy responses. The challenges of attribution, jurisdictional conflicts, and balancing privacy with security further complicate efforts to combat cybercrime effectively. Addressing these challenges requires a multi-faceted approach that includes strengthening legal frameworks, fostering public–private partnerships, enhancing international cooperation, and investing in cybersecurity education and infrastructure.

Chapter 5
The Influence of National Socio-Economic Background on Victimization: A Cross-Country Analysis

5.1 Introduction

Victimization is a global phenomenon that transcends national boundaries, social structures, and legal systems. While crime and victimhood manifest in diverse forms across the world, the underlying socio-economic conditions in which individuals and communities exist remain a critical determinant of their vulnerability to crime. The intersection of poverty, inequality, limited access to education, and social exclusion often contributes to heightened risks of victimization, particularly in regions experiencing economic instability or systemic underdevelopment. At the same time, nations with greater socio-economic resources may encounter different patterns of crime and victimization, shaped by distinct institutional, technological, and demographic factors.

Understanding the role of socio-economic background in shaping victimization is essential for the development of effective prevention strategies, equitable public policy, and responsive victim services. Numerous international studies have pointed to strong correlations between socio-economic disadvantage and elevated crime rates, particularly for offenses involving violence, exploitation, and interpersonal harm. The United Nations Office on Drugs and Crime (UNODC) and the International Crime Victims Survey (ICVS) have consistently reported disparities in victimization rates across countries, underscoring the influence of income inequality, unemployment, and education levels on individuals' exposure to crime.

In this chapter, we adopt a comparative international framework to examine how national socio-economic contexts affect the likelihood, nature, and experience of victimization. By analyzing a diverse sample of countries, including the United States, Germany, Canada, Japan, Brazil, India, Bangladesh, Nigeria, and Haiti, we aim to identify patterns that illustrate both the universality and specificity of victimization risks in different cultural, economic, and legal environments. This approach facilitates a nuanced understanding of the ways in which systemic factors shape victimization beyond individual or situational determinants.

M. K. A. Lukings et al., *Understanding Cybercrime Victim Services*, Progress in IS,
https://doi.org/10.1007/978-3-032-13273-4_5

Our research objectives are fourfold: (1) to explore theoretical frameworks that explain the socio-economic roots of victimization; (2) to outline a methodology for conducting cross-national comparisons using standardized economic and crime indicators; (3) to analyze empirical data across countries with varying income levels; and (4) to draw evidence-based conclusions about the impact of social policies, law enforcement strategies, and economic reforms on victimization rates. The analysis will also highlight successful crime reduction models, regional trends, and policy implications for strengthening victim services in diverse socio-economic contexts.

By situating cybercrime victimization within broader socio-economic structures, this chapter builds upon previous discussions and continues the textbook's emphasis on contextual, systemic, and evidence-informed perspectives. In doing so, it seeks to contribute to an expanded global understanding of how social inequality, economic development, and governance frameworks shape both the prevalence and experience of victimization in the digital age and beyond.

5.2 Theoretical Framework

Understanding the relationship between socio-economic conditions and victimization requires a foundation in criminological theory that considers both individual behavior and broader structural forces. Two of the most widely applied and enduring theories in this area are Strain Theory and Routine Activity Theory. These models offer distinct yet complementary perspectives on how poverty, inequality, and social exclusion contribute to crime and victimization. Together, they help illuminate the complex mechanisms through which structural disadvantage shapes both offending and vulnerability to harm.

5.2.1 Strain Theory

Strain Theory, first introduced by Robert K. Merton in the 1930s and later expanded by others, is grounded in the idea that societal structures, especially economic and cultural systems, exert pressure on individuals that can lead to criminal behavior. Merton proposed that every society promotes certain culturally approved goals (e.g., wealth, success, status), but does not provide equal access to the legitimate means of achieving them (e.g., education, employment). When individuals are unable to achieve these goals through socially acceptable avenues, they may experience strain, frustration, or alienation, which can lead to deviance, including criminal activity.

Merton identified five modes of adaptation to this strain:

- **Conformity**: Accepting societal goals and the means to achieve them.
- **Innovation**: Accepting the goals but using illegitimate or criminal means (e.g., theft, fraud).

- **Ritualism**: Abandoning the goals but rigidly adhering to the rules.
- **Retreatism**: Rejecting both goals and means (e.g., drug addiction, vagrancy).
- **Rebellion**: Creating new goals and means through revolutionary behavior.

For the purposes of victimization analysis, Strain Theory helps explain not only the motivations of offenders, but also the unequal exposure to risk experienced by individuals and communities. Those living in economically marginalized environments are more likely to experience strain due to limited educational, occupational, and social mobility. This, in turn, increases both the likelihood of criminal behavior and the risk of victimization, as such environments may foster more frequent criminal incidents and weaker protective institutions (e.g., under-resourced policing or limited victim services).

Modern interpretations of Strain Theory, including General Strain Theory (GST) by Robert Agnew, extend the concept beyond economic goals. GST considers other sources of strain, such as loss of positive stimuli (e.g., job loss, relationship breakdown) or exposure to negative stimuli (e.g., abuse, discrimination). These strains can elicit negative emotions like anger or despair, increasing the likelihood of deviant coping mechanisms, especially when legitimate coping resources are unavailable.

Strain Theory remains especially useful in explaining patterns of crime and victimization in low- and middle-income contexts, where large populations are structurally excluded from economic success, and in urban centers within wealthy nations where marginalized communities exist alongside extreme wealth, exacerbating feelings of relative deprivation.

5.2.2 *Routine Activity Theory*

Routine Activity Theory (RAT), formulated by **Lawrence Cohen and Marcus Felson** in 1979, shifts the focus from social strain to the **situational and environmental conditions** that facilitate crime. According to RAT, crime occurs when three elements converge at a specific time and place:

1. **A motivated offender**
2. **A suitable target**
3. **The absence of a capable guardian**

This deceptively simple framework has proven highly influential in both academic research and crime prevention policy. Rather than emphasizing why individuals become criminals, RAT focuses on the **opportunity structures** that make crime possible, suggesting that criminal events are largely shaped by **patterns in everyday life**, or routine activities.

RAT emphasizes that socio-economic conditions can significantly influence all three elements of the crime triangle:

- **Motivated offenders** may be more prevalent in areas of concentrated disadvantage, where poverty, unemployment, and social disorganization increase incentives for criminal behavior.
- **Suitable targets** are shaped by environmental and economic context. In low-income areas, homes or businesses may lack proper security measures, while individuals may be more exposed in public spaces due to reliance on walking or public transit.
- **Capable guardians**, including police, security systems, neighbors, and even digital safeguards, are often weaker or absent in impoverished communities.

A helpful extension of RAT is the **VIVA model**, which describes what makes a target suitable for victimization:

- **Value**: The monetary or personal worth of the item or person targeted.
- **Inertia**: The physical characteristics that influence how easily an object can be stolen or moved.
- **Visibility**: The extent to which a target is exposed or noticeable to offenders.
- **Access**: The ease with which an offender can approach or reach the target.

This model applies equally well to physical and digital spaces. In the context of **cybercrime**, for example, victims may be those whose online activities lack adequate guardianship (e.g., no antivirus software, weak passwords) and whose data or financial resources are visible and valuable to offenders.

Routine Activity Theory is especially valuable in explaining **how socio-economic disparities create risky environments**. Poor neighborhoods often suffer from under-policing, broken infrastructure, and overcrowded housing, all of which increase criminal opportunities. Additionally, individuals in these settings may have routines that require being in vulnerable spaces at vulnerable times, such as walking long distances after dark due to lack of transit.

RAT also helps explain trends in **targeted crime**, such as burglary, car theft, and street robbery, as well as more complex offenses like cyber fraud and stalking. Importantly, the theory has contributed to the development of **situational crime prevention strategies**, including improved street lighting, surveillance cameras, neighborhood watch programs, and digital literacy campaigns.

5.2.3 Conclusion

A growing body of cross-national research affirms the connection between social inequality and victimization. Studies consistently show that individuals living in economically marginalized areas face a greater risk of both violent and property crimes. Poverty and unemployment are associated not only with increased rates of offending but also with reduced access to protective institutions such as effective law enforcement, victim services, and secure housing. Moreover, income inequality itself, not merely poverty, has been linked to higher levels of fear, insecurity, and victimization, even in otherwise affluent societies.

Beyond theoretical models, empirical evidence also underscores the importance of socio-economic context in shaping crime patterns. For example, comparative studies of bullying and interpersonal violence reveal that adolescents from lower socio-economic backgrounds are more likely to experience peer victimization. A meta-analysis by Tippett and Wolke (2014) of 28 studies confirmed that children from low-income households had a significantly higher likelihood of being involved in bullying, either as victims or bully-victims, compared to their wealthier peers. These results highlight the powerful influence of socio-economic disadvantage on interpersonal violence and victimization during formative years.

Adding to this, Due et al. (2009) analyzed data from 35 countries and found a strong relationship between national income inequality and school bullying. A 10-point increase in national income inequality (measured by the GINI coefficient) was associated with a 34% higher likelihood of frequent bullying among students, even after controlling for individual SES, gender, and age. This underscores how macro-level inequality amplifies risks of victimization independently of personal circumstances, reinforcing the idea that structural disparities normalize or facilitate harmful behaviors in schools. These findings lend further support to theoretical models emphasizing the role of structural and situational factors in shaping victimization risk.

In sum, this theoretical framework provides the foundation for our cross-country analysis by establishing a link between economic conditions and victimization risks. While individual factors such as age, gender, and behavior undoubtedly play a role, they must be understood within the broader social structures that influence both opportunities for crime and the availability of protective mechanisms. By situating our inquiry within these well-established and evolving theories, we aim to better understand how national socio-economic backgrounds shape victimization patterns on a global scale.

Together, Strain Theory and Routine Activity Theory offer distinct but complementary insights, one emphasizing structural inequality and motivation, the other focusing on environmental conditions and opportunity. By incorporating both models, we gain a more holistic understanding of how socio-economic forces shape victimization across global contexts.

5.3 Methodology

A rigorous and systematic methodology is essential for conducting a cross-national analysis of socio-economic background and its influence on victimization. This section outlines the criteria for country selection, the sources of data, the key variables used in comparative analysis, and the general framework for clustering countries based on economic development levels. Together, these components form the foundation for the subsequent empirical and case study sections of this chapter.

5.3.1 Selection Criteria for Countries

The selection of countries for this analysis was guided by the need to capture a broad spectrum of socio-economic conditions and legal-political systems. To ensure diversity and relevance, we selected ten countries, United States, Germany, Canada, Japan, Brazil, India, Bangladesh, Nigeria, Haiti, and South Africa, based on the following criteria:

- **Economic diversity**: Inclusion of high-, middle-, and low-income nations, as classified by the World Bank.
- **Geographic and cultural variation**: Representation from North America, Europe, Latin America, Asia, and Africa to provide a global perspective.
- **Availability of reliable data**: Countries for which consistent data on socio-economic indicators and crime statistics are available through reputable sources such as the UNODC and the World Bank.
- **Relevance to cybercrime and victimization**: Countries with documented challenges and trends in cybercrime, interpersonal violence, and systemic victimization.

This diverse selection enables a comparative approach that highlights both universal and context-specific patterns of victimization.

5.3.2 Data Sources

Data were collected from a range of globally recognized and statistically rigorous sources, including:

- **United Nations Office on Drugs and Crime (UNODC):** For national crime statistics, including rates of homicide, robbery, and other forms of interpersonal violence.
- **World Bank Indicators:** For socio-economic variables such as GDP per capita, education levels, unemployment rates, and GINI coefficients.
- **International Crime Victims Survey (ICVS) and national victimization surveys (where available):** For direct measures of victim experiences, reporting behavior, and perceptions of safety.

While these sources provide valuable insights, it is important to acknowledge their methodological limitations. As noted in both Kalish's (1988) comparative study of crime rates and United Nations methodological reports, crime statistics are often shaped by variations in legal definitions, reporting behavior, and data collection processes across countries. For instance, what qualifies as "assault" or "rape" in one jurisdiction may be defined differently elsewhere, making direct comparisons between countries problematic.

Moreover, official crime data typically represent only the crimes reported to and recorded by authorities, and are influenced by factors such as public trust in law enforcement, accessibility of police services, cultural stigma (especially in cases of sexual violence), and insurance-related incentives for reporting. Victimization surveys such as the ICVS attempt to address these gaps, but still encounter issues related to sampling, recall accuracy, and cultural context.

In support of this multi-source data approach, Kizilgol and Selim (2017) conducted a panel count data analysis of the EU 28 and Turkey using fixed-effects negative binomial regression. Their study confirms that official cross-national datasets, when used cautiously, can reveal meaningful structural relationships between socio-economic indicators and crime rates, specifically, the authors found strong statistical links between crime and variables such as GDP per capita, unemployment, and urban density. They also noted the protective impact of education enrollment and police presence, reinforcing the value of including such variables in cross-national analysis.

5.3.3 Key Variables

The study employs a set of variables that reflect both socio-economic background and crime/victimization dynamics. These include:

- **GDP per capita**: As a proxy for overall economic development and resource availability.
- **Education levels**: Measured by average years of schooling and school enrollment rates.
- **Unemployment rates**: Including both general unemployment and youth-specific rates.
- **Income inequality**: Represented by the GINI index, which reflects the distribution of income within a population.
- **Crime statistics**: Including reported rates of homicide, robbery, assault, and cybercrime where data permits.

While homicide data are generally considered more reliable and comparable across jurisdictions, other crime types, such as assault, sexual violence, or cybercrime, are often subject to significant underreporting or definitional divergence, as highlighted in the UN's framework on cross-national data. Thus, findings involving such offenses must be interpreted with caution.

5.3.4 Comparative Approach

To facilitate meaningful comparisons, countries were grouped into three broad categories based on World Bank classifications:

- **High-income countries** (e.g., United States, Germany, Canada, Japan)
- **Middle-income countries** (e.g., Brazil, India, South Africa)
- **Low-income countries** (e.g., Bangladesh, Nigeria, Haiti)

This clustering allows for the analysis of how different levels of economic development shape the forms and frequency of victimization. It also enables a clearer understanding of how state capacity, public policy, and access to services influence the effectiveness of responses to crime and victimhood.

That said, experts consistently caution against overly simplistic comparisons of reported crime rates across countries. As both Kalish (1988) and the UN (2022) emphasize, cross-national comparisons are methodologically challenging due to three primary issues:

1. **Different legal definitions** for the same crime types;
2. **Varying levels of crime reporting and law enforcement practices**, often tied to development and trust in institutions;
3. **Cultural, political, and economic context**, which influences both the likelihood of crime occurring and the willingness of victims to report it.

Rather than using these data to rank countries by crime levels, the focus of this chapter, and the broader international datasets it draws on, is to explore patterns, policy responses, and socio-economic risk factors in context. The UN's crime surveys are best used to examine trends within countries over time and to assess governmental responses to crime, rather than to provide absolute measures of criminal activity.

The comparative approach adopted in this chapter is thus both descriptive and analytical. While descriptive statistics provide an overview of crime and socio-economic indicators, the analysis emphasizes structural patterns and institutional contexts that inform policy development and victim support services. This method acknowledges the imperfections in the data, while still enabling valuable insights into the socio-economic determinants of victimization worldwide.

5.4 Socio-Economic Background and Victimization: A Cross-National Analysis

Socio-economic background plays a pivotal role in shaping patterns of victimization across different national contexts. By examining crime rates and victimization experiences in countries with varying levels of income and development, we can begin to understand how structural inequalities influence both the risk and the nature of criminal victimization. This section presents a comparative overview of victimization trends in high-, middle-, and low-income countries, focusing on how economic disparity, public policy, and institutional effectiveness impact victim experiences and outcomes.

5.4.1 Developed Countries: Trends in High-Income Nations

High-income countries such as the United States, Germany, Canada, Japan, and many members of the European Union have experienced varying crime trends over the past two decades. While overall crime rates in these countries have tended to decline, particularly in terms of property offenses, significant challenges remain, particularly in urban centers marked by economic inequality, demographic shifts, and systemic underinvestment in vulnerable communities.

For instance, in 2021, the United States recorded the highest homicide rate among G7 nations, at 6.81 per 100,000 inhabitants, whereas Japan reported the lowest, with only 0.23 per 100,000 (Statista). In Canada, crime tends to be concentrated in areas facing economic marginalization and housing insecurity, and in Germany, migrant and refugee populations report disproportionately high rates of victimization and fear of crime. Despite the availability of victim services in these nations, barriers to access, including language, legal status, and institutional trust, continue to shape victim outcomes.

Further insight into crime trends within the European context is provided by Kizilgol and Selim's (2017) panel count data analysis of the EU 28 countries and Turkey. Using fixed effects negative binomial regression on data from 2001 to 2010, the authors found that GDP per capita, unemployment rate, and urban overpopulation were all positively and significantly associated with increases in recorded crime rates. In contrast, higher education enrollment rates and a greater number of police officers were correlated with reductions in crime. These findings underscore the complex dynamics at play in high-income regions, where economic growth does not uniformly lead to safer communities unless coupled with social investments in education and public safety infrastructure.

The study also reinforces a key trend observed across high-income countries: urbanization is a consistent predictor of increased crime, particularly in contexts where public services are overburdened or unevenly distributed. As cities grow and economic pressures mount, the risk of victimization may rise, especially among marginalized groups who lack access to secure housing, reliable income, or supportive institutions.

Overall, while high-income countries benefit from more extensive criminal justice systems and victim services compared to their lower-income counterparts, the distribution and effectiveness of these resources remain uneven. The persistence of socio-economic disparities, even within advanced economies, continues to shape who becomes a victim, what support they receive, and how justice is ultimately experienced.

5.4.2 *Emerging Economies: Victimization Patterns in Middle-Income Countries*

Emerging economies such as Brazil, South Africa, India, and Pakistan demonstrate complex and often contradictory crime dynamics shaped by rapid economic development, population growth, and persistent socio-economic inequality. These countries face significant challenges in managing both traditional forms of interpersonal violence and emerging threats such as cybercrime and organized crime. The vulnerability of populations in these nations is often exacerbated by inconsistent access to education, high unemployment, and under-resourced law enforcement institutions.

In Brazil, for example, over one million homicides occurred between 1980 and 2010, with contributing factors including widening income inequality, the proliferation of firearms, and drug-related violence (PubMed Central). Similarly, South Africa continues to report high rates of violent crime, which have been linked to enduring social inequities and limited institutional capacity to provide protection in underserved communities (World Bank).

A comparative econometric study of India and Pakistan (Aboya et al., 2022) adds empirical depth to the analysis of victimization in South Asia. The study analyzed time-series data from 1996 to 2020 using an ARDL (Autoregressive Distributed Lag) model and found that poverty and education are the most influential socio-economic determinants of crime in both countries. In Pakistan, higher levels of education were significantly associated with reduced crime rates in both the short and long term. Poverty, on the other hand, was consistently found to increase crime, underscoring the role of economic deprivation in fostering criminal behavior.

In India, the findings were more nuanced. While no long-term relationship between socio-economic variables and crime was statistically significant, poverty was found to be a key short-run driver of crime, and education also exhibited a short-term crime-reducing effect. These results reflect both countries' shared challenges, such as high rates of urban poverty and underemployment, as well as the limits of macroeconomic growth to translate into meaningful social protection. Notably, the study found no consistent link between unemployment and crime, highlighting the complexity of informal labor dynamics and possibly under-reported crime in certain contexts.

Together, these examples illustrate that in many emerging economies, economic growth alone is insufficient to reduce crime and victimization. Without parallel investments in education, poverty reduction, and institutional reform, socio-economic disparities continue to expose large segments of the population to heightened risk. In the context of global victim services, these findings reinforce the importance of targeted, equity-focused interventions in middle-income countries navigating rapid social change.

5.4.3 Low-Income Nations: Crime Vulnerability in Developing Regions

In low-income countries such as Nigeria, Bangladesh, and Haiti, economic hardship, political instability, and weak institutional capacity contribute to persistent victimization. In Nigeria, early exposure to violence is a key predictor of future offending, indicating a cyclical nature of victimization that spans generations (CDC). Victim services are often minimal or absent, and access to justice is hindered by corruption, resource shortages, and lack of public trust in law enforcement.

Bangladesh, though experiencing economic growth, remains vulnerable to politically motivated violence, gender-based crime, and organized crime in urban slums. Data limitations and underreporting challenge the assessment of victimization, but structural vulnerabilities such as overcrowding, poor infrastructure, and limited legal recourse amplify risks (World Bank).

In Haiti, chronic poverty, natural disasters, and fragile governance contribute to a pervasive climate of insecurity. Armed gangs, political violence, and extortion disproportionately affect impoverished neighborhoods, where state institutions are largely absent. Victims are often left without any form of redress or protection (World Bank).

5.4.4 Role of Social Policies, Law Enforcement, and Economic Stability

Across all national contexts, effective social policies and institutional capacity significantly influence victimization outcomes. Countries that invest in education, social welfare, and equitable law enforcement tend to report lower crime rates and higher levels of public trust. For example, targeted youth employment programs and community policing initiatives in parts of Latin America have contributed to localized reductions in violence. In contrast, nations lacking social safety nets or facing high levels of corruption often struggle to respond to victimization or prevent its recurrence.

Economic stability also plays a preventive role. As demonstrated in several studies, countries with higher GDP growth and lower unemployment tend to experience reduced rates of crime. However, economic development alone is insufficient. Without accompanying investments in justice infrastructure, education, and healthcare, socio-economic progress may fail to translate into improved safety or victim outcomes.

This cross-national analysis illustrates that while victimization is a global concern, the socio-economic conditions under which individuals live play a defining role in determining who becomes a victim, what forms that victimization takes, and how effectively society can respond.

5.5 Case Studies and Regional Comparisons

To deepen the understanding of how socio-economic contexts shape victimization across the globe, this section presents regional comparisons and case-specific insights. By analyzing the interplay between economic disparity, institutional response, and crime trends in different geographic and cultural settings, we highlight the variability in victimization risks and the effectiveness of policy responses. These regional comparisons also reveal broader patterns of inequality and systemic disadvantage that inform both local and global efforts to address victimization.

5.5.1 Europe vs. Latin America: The Impact of Economic Disparity

Although both Europe and Latin America encompass a wide range of economic conditions and cultural contexts, comparisons between the two regions offer valuable insights into how economic disparity and structural inequality shape victimization trends. Latin America is widely recognized as one of the most unequal regions in the world, with the top 10% of earners earning, on average, twelve times more than the bottom 10%. This entrenched inequality is directly associated with elevated rates of violent crime, particularly among lower-income populations who are disproportionately affected by homicide, assault, and robbery (IADB).

In contrast, while most European countries enjoy relatively higher income levels and more extensive social welfare systems, socio-economic variables still exert a significant influence on crime patterns. According to a comparative study by Kizilgol and Selim (2017), which examined crime determinants across the EU 28 countries and Turkey from 2001 to 2010, several socio-economic indicators were found to be strongly associated with crime rates. Specifically, GDP per capita, unemployment, and urban overpopulation were positively linked to increased crime, while education (enrollment rates) and the presence of law enforcement (number of police officers) were linked to reductions in recorded crime.

These findings suggest that while European countries may differ from Latin America in overall crime rates and institutional capacity, the underlying dynamics, particularly the role of economic stressors and urban inequality, are strikingly similar. Urban centers in both regions face heightened crime risks where social supports are lacking or unevenly distributed, and the presence or absence of proactive policy responses can significantly affect outcomes.

The role of redistributive social policy also helps explain the divergence in crime outcomes across the two regions. As Cornia (2011) found, Latin America, particularly Brazil, witnessed a decline in income inequality during the early 2000s due to the implementation of robust redistributive measures. Conditional cash transfers, minimum wage hikes, and expanded access to education helped mitigate the negative distributional effects of globalization and trade liberalization. These welfare strategies not only improved equity but also supported broader social cohesion, indirectly contributing to reductions in violence and victimization. In contrast, many European economies in transition saw a rise in inequality during the same period, often due to weaker redistributive mechanisms and fragmented welfare systems.

These updated studies highlight that inequality is not static; it fluctuates based on historical and geographic factors. For example, while Brazil and Peru saw reductions in inequality from the 1980s to 2010, Costa Rica's inequality steadily increased during the same period. Wealth inequality has proven to be even more severe than income inequality, with many low-income households experiencing negative net worth.

Crucially, the intergenerational transmission of inequality, whether through inherited disadvantage, ethnic discrimination, or geographic segregation, further exacerbates vulnerability to crime. Policy recommendations from the IDB and scholars such as Cornia emphasize the importance of adaptive, evidence-based strategies that go beyond traditional approaches. While education and cash transfers remain important tools, they must be complemented by reforms in fiscal policy, labor markets, and social protections to prevent victimization effectively..

5.5.2 North America vs. Africa: Crime Types and Socio-Economic Influences

North America and Africa illustrate differing manifestations of socio-economic influences on crime. In North America, crime tends to be concentrated in economically disadvantaged urban areas, with systemic issues such as racial segregation, housing inequality, and underfunded education systems contributing to persistent victimization. Research from Canada's Department of Justice emphasizes that even within prosperous cities, crime and victimization are unevenly distributed along socio-economic lines.

Evidence from the United States further reinforces the role of early education investment in reducing crime. A longitudinal study by Baron, Hyman, and Vasquez (2022), affiliated with the University of Michigan's Gerald R. Ford School of Public Policy, found that students who attended better-funded public elementary schools were 15% less likely to be arrested by age 30. The researchers linked this outcome to higher teacher experience, smaller class sizes, and improved behavioral and academic performance. Crucially, they determined that the social savings from reduced adult crime outweighed the costs of the increased education funding, illustrating the crime prevention benefits of robust and equitable public school investments.

In many African nations, such as Nigeria and South Africa, crime is closely tied to poverty, limited state capacity, and post-colonial socio-political instability. The UNODC reports that weak rule of law, under-resourced policing, and high unemployment contribute to a variety of crimes including interpersonal violence, human trafficking, and organized criminal activity. The absence of effective legal and victim support infrastructures leaves many victims without meaningful recourse. In contrast to North America, where institutional responses are more robust, if unevenly distributed, victims in parts of Africa often face both systemic neglect and active re-victimization by corrupt authorities or armed groups.

5.5.3 Asian Countries: Cybercrime, Human Trafficking, and Economic Disparities

Asia presents a complex interplay of technological advancement and socio-economic disparity. Countries such as India, Bangladesh, and parts of Southeast Asia face a dual challenge: the rapid expansion of digital connectivity alongside persistent poverty and inequality. This context creates fertile ground for cybercrime, where victims often lack digital literacy and institutional protection. In wealthier nations like Japan and South Korea, cybersecurity infrastructure is more advanced, but victims of online harassment and digital fraud still report underwhelming institutional responses.

Human trafficking remains a major issue across South and Southeast Asia, disproportionately affecting women and children from lower socio-economic backgrounds. Poverty, lack of education, and regional migration all contribute to vulnerability. Despite legal frameworks against trafficking, enforcement remains weak in many jurisdictions, and victim support services are often inaccessible or stigmatized.

5.5.4 Countries with Successful Crime Reduction Strategies

Some countries, particularly in Latin America and Europe, have implemented innovative policy measures that have successfully reduced crime and improved victim outcomes. In Latin America, despite its overall high crime rates, localized successes have emerged through targeted social programs. For instance, community-based interventions focusing on youth employment, education access, and conflict mediation in cities like Medellín, Colombia, have shown measurable declines in homicide rates and increased public trust in authorities (Desapublications).

In Europe, countries with strong social welfare systems and inclusive economic policies, such as those in Scandinavia, exhibit some of the lowest crime rates globally. Comparative studies suggest that social cohesion, universal access to healthcare and education, and robust labor protections contribute to both lower victimization rates and higher satisfaction with justice processes (SpringerLink). These models demonstrate that sustained investments in social infrastructure can mitigate the effects of inequality and reduce crime in meaningful, long-term ways.

5.6 Discussion and Policy Implications

The comparative analysis presented in this chapter reveals a clear and compelling link between national socio-economic conditions and the prevalence and nature of victimization. Across diverse contexts, from high-income countries with advanced institutional frameworks to developing nations facing chronic poverty and weak governance, socio-economic inequality emerges as a consistent driver of victimization risk. This section synthesizes key findings, examines the impact of government policies and reforms, considers the role of social welfare programs, and outlines future research directions and policy recommendations.

5.6.1 Key Findings from International Comparisons

One of the most consistent findings across regions is that socio-economic disadvantage correlates strongly with elevated crime rates and victimization, particularly for violent offenses such as homicide, assault, and robbery. As confirmed by numerous national and international studies, communities with lower income, less education, and higher unemployment are more likely to experience both crime and systemic underprotection. However, recent comparative analyses also highlight the complex and at times contradictory nature of these relationships, depending on local economic and institutional contexts.

For example, the Kizilgol and Selim (2017) study of the EU 28 and Turkey found that GDP per capita, unemployment, and urban overpopulation were all positively correlated with increased crime rates during the 2001–2010 period. While economic growth is often assumed to reduce crime, their findings suggest that urban pressures and inequality within wealthy regions may actually elevate victimization risks, especially where public infrastructure is strained. At the same time, the study reinforces the protective impact of education and law enforcement resources, showing that increased enrollment rates and a higher number of police officers were associated with lower crime rates across the region. These results were produced using fixed-effects negative binomial regression, offering a robust methodological complement to the time-series econometric approach used in the South Asian case studies reviewed earlier in the chapter.

These findings, along with others reviewed in this chapter, reaffirm that crime and victimization are shaped not simply by economic level but by how resources are distributed, how populations are concentrated, and how governments respond to emerging social risks. Both relative and absolute deprivation matter, and where gaps in education, housing, or safety widen, so too do patterns of victimization.

5.6.2 Impact of Government Policies, Education, and Economic Reforms

Government policies have a decisive influence on both the root causes of crime and the effectiveness of victimization prevention and response strategies. Across the countries examined in this chapter, policies focused on education access, employment creation, and income redistribution have proven particularly effective in mitigating the socio-economic drivers of crime. However, the outcomes of these policies vary depending on how they are designed, implemented, and integrated with broader social systems.

The comparative study of Pakistan and India by Aboya et al. (2022) offers clear evidence that education and poverty alleviation policies can yield measurable crime reduction benefits. In Pakistan, the study found that increased levels of education significantly reduce crime, both in the short and long term. This reinforces the argument that expanding access to quality education can serve as a powerful preventative tool, not only by enhancing employment prospects but also by fostering social cohesion and reducing marginalization. In India, the relationship between education and crime was more pronounced in the short term, suggesting that immediate gains from education initiatives, such as skills training or secondary school completion, may help lower crime rates in the near future, even if structural barriers persist in the long run.

The same study also identified poverty as a consistent driver of crime, particularly in Pakistan. This finding supports broader literature linking economic deprivation to increased victimization risk, especially in environments where social safety nets are weak or inconsistently applied. Policymakers in both countries are therefore urged to design interventions that target the distributional outcomes of economic growth, ensuring that gains reach the most vulnerable segments of the population.

Furthermore, the study's inconclusive findings regarding unemployment challenge assumptions that joblessness alone explains crime trends. This suggests a need for more nuanced, context-specific economic policies that address underemployment, informal labor, and precarious work conditions, factors often masked by headline employment statistics.

Additional insights come from Kizilgol and Selim's (2017) panel data analysis of the EU 28 countries and Turkey, which examined the socio-economic and demographic determinants of crime across a high-income and urbanized context. Their study found that higher GDP per capita, unemployment, and urban overpopulation were significantly associated with increased crime rates, highlighting that economic development alone does not guarantee public safety. Crucially, they also found that increased education enrollment and a greater number of police officers were significantly correlated with reductions in crime, reinforcing the role of both human capital investment and public safety infrastructure in reducing victimization.

New longitudinal evidence from the United States further strengthens the case for educational policy as a crime prevention strategy. A study by Baron, Hyman, and Vasquez (2022) tracked two cohorts of students from kindergarten into adulthood and found that those who attended better-funded elementary schools were 15% less likely to be arrested by age 30. These students benefited from more experienced teachers, smaller class sizes, and more administrative support. The authors attributed the reduction in adult crime to improved academic and behavioral outcomes, as well as increased educational attainment. Importantly, they found that the social savings generated by reductions in crime exceeded the cost of the initial education investment, providing a powerful economic rationale for early, equitable public school funding as a long-term public safety strategy.

Additional empirical validation comes from a recent U.S.-based study by Jason Vargas (2023), which analyzed state-level data to assess how education, income, and unemployment interact to influence crime rates. The study found a strong inverse correlation between high school graduation rates and property crime, and between higher education levels and violent crime. It also showed that while median income is negatively correlated with crime, the most consistent predictors emerged when education, income, and employment variables were analyzed together. Vargas concluded that educational attainment remains the most powerful protective factor, particularly when accompanied by economic stability and reduced inequality. These findings support a multifactoral policy approach to crime prevention, one that integrates educational investment, equitable income distribution, and labor market inclusion.

Supporting this, Foley (2008) demonstrated that even the structure and timing of welfare distribution can significantly impact crime trends. Using daily crime data from twelve U.S. cities, Foley found that jurisdictions issuing welfare payments in a lump sum at the beginning of each month experienced notable spikes in economically motivated crimes, such as burglary and robbery, later in the month. In contrast, cities with staggered or more frequent payment schedules did not exhibit such patterns. This suggests that the design of welfare systems, including payment frequency, can help mitigate short-term financial desperation and reduce related criminal behavior. Foley's findings, grounded in behavioral economics, highlight that many individuals display short-run impatience in consumption patterns. When funds are exhausted and access to credit or savings is limited, crime may emerge as an alternative. As such, welfare reform, when informed by behavioral insights, can function as both a poverty alleviation and crime prevention strategy.

Routine Activity Theory also provides an important lens for understanding how environmental conditions and policy frameworks shape victimization risk. As outlined in the literature, crime is more likely to occur when a motivated offender encounters a suitable target in the absence of a capable guardian. Socio-economic conditions, particularly those that influence daily routines and exposure, play a vital role in determining whether these three elements converge. For instance, in economically disadvantaged neighborhoods with poor lighting, inadequate policing, and overcrowded housing, residents are more likely to encounter unsafe conditions that elevate the risk of victimization. Public policies that improve urban infrastructure, expand community policing, and increase access to safe spaces can disrupt these opportunity structures.

Research from Simply Psychology (2024) reinforces this perspective, highlighting how adjustments to routine activities, such as the implementation of neighborhood watch programs, better lighting, and increased digital literacy, can reduce both the opportunity for crime and the fear of victimization. These policy tools, grounded in Routine Activity Theory, are particularly important in urban environments where socio-economic vulnerabilities are concentrated.

5.6.3 *Influence of Social Welfare Programs on Victimization Rates*

Social welfare programs serve as critical buffers against crime by addressing root causes of vulnerability such as poverty, lack of education, and social exclusion. By providing essential resources and promoting stability, these programs can directly reduce both the incidence of crime and individuals' risk of victimization. Across national contexts, the structure, reach, and quality of welfare systems significantly influence not only who becomes a victim but also how, and whether, victims are supported in the aftermath of crime.

In their comparative analysis of Pakistan and India, Aboya et al. (2022) found that poverty was one of the most consistent predictors of crime, with higher levels of deprivation associated with increased rates of offending. In Pakistan, education was found to significantly reduce crime in both the short and long term. These findings support the broader understanding that targeted investments in education and poverty alleviation are not only developmental priorities but also powerful tools of crime prevention. In India, while the long-term statistical associations were weaker, short-term gains from educational access were linked to decreased crime rates, underscoring the need for sustained and equitable implementation of welfare policies.

These results are mirrored in high-income contexts as well. In their panel data analysis of EU 28 countries and Turkey, Kizilgol and Selim (2017) found that higher education enrollment rates and greater numbers of police officers were significantly associated with reduced crime rates. Importantly, their study also indicated that urban overpopulation and higher GDP per capita, when not accompanied by equitable social spending, were linked to increased crime. This suggests that economic growth alone is not a sufficient safeguard against rising victimization unless it is matched by adequate social infrastructure and redistributive policies.

A particularly relevant comparative study by Cornia (2011) examined inequality and growth trajectories in Latin America and the European transition economies. His findings underscore how differences in social policy responses to globalization produced divergent inequality outcomes across these regions. In Latin America, particularly in Brazil, inequality declined during the early 2000s, driven by active redistributive measures such as conditional cash transfers, minimum wage hikes, and expanded education access. These programs mitigated the adverse distributional effects of trade liberalization and capital mobility, showing that robust welfare strategies can effectively counteract the inequality typically associated with globalization.

By contrast, many European economies in transition saw rising inequality during the same period, in part due to weaker redistributive institutions and less comprehensive welfare policies. Cornia's analysis reinforces the argument that inclusive social spending, especially when directed toward education and income redistribution, can both reduce inequality and lower victimization risk. His work offers compelling evidence that the design and political prioritization of welfare programs matter deeply in shaping socio-economic outcomes.

Both studies reinforce the argument that social welfare interventions must be context-sensitive. In lower-income countries, where institutional reach may be limited, even modest welfare programs can have meaningful effects on reducing victimization by improving access to education, healthcare, or food security. In higher-income settings, welfare programs must go beyond subsistence to address inequality, urban density, and service accessibility, factors that significantly impact perceived and actual safety.

The policy implications are clear: well-designed welfare systems contribute not only to individual wellbeing but also to broader public safety outcomes. Social investments that reduce inequality, support early education, and ensure access to secure housing and employment can serve as upstream interventions that prevent victimization before it occurs. Conversely, when such systems are absent, underfunded, or unequally distributed, populations are left more vulnerable to the structural drivers of crime.

Further evidence of the protective role of social and educational investment can be found in the large-scale study conducted by Due et al. (2009), which examined school bullying in 35 countries. The study found that students living in countries with higher national income inequality were significantly more likely to be victims of bullying, even after adjusting for personal socioeconomic status and demographic factors. Specifically, a 10-point increase in a country's GINI coefficient was associated with a 34% increase in frequent bullying. These findings suggest that broad societal inequities can permeate school environments, increasing victimization risk in ways not explained by individual disadvantage alone. As such, school-based anti-bullying programs and inclusive social policies must take into account the wider context of economic inequality and structural vulnerability.

Additional evidence from a national context with persistent inequality is found in the work of Murray, Cerqueira, and Kahn (2013), who conducted a systematic review of violent crime and its risk factors in Brazil between 1980 and 2010. Despite notable gains in education and health services, Brazil experienced over one million homicides during the study period. The authors identified structural inequality, poverty, and institutional exclusion, particularly in urban peripheries, as key drivers of persistent violence. They also noted that while Brazil's prison population increased dramatically, this punitive trend did not correspond to a measurable reduction in victimization. Instead, the review emphasized the need for sustained investment in early childhood education, youth engagement programs, and inclusive urban development as more effective strategies to prevent crime. These findings reinforce the view that crime prevention is most effective when it is embedded within broader frameworks of social equity and developmental policy.

Further empirical support for the link between economic vulnerability and increased victimization comes from the Global Pulse initiative's cross-national analysis conducted by the United Nations Office on Drugs and Crime (UNODC) in the GIVAS Final Report (2011). This study analyzed monthly time-series crime and economic data across 15 countries and cities, focusing particularly on the global financial crisis of 2008–2009. It found that economic downturns were often associated with significant increases in specific types of crime, especially violent property crimes such as robbery. In some cases, these increases reached up to double pre-crisis levels.

Crucially, the study demonstrated that 80% of the countries analyzed showed statistically significant associations between economic variables (such as unemployment, real income, and share price indices) and crime rates, most often with a lag of several months. These patterns support the notion that economic stress, when unbuffered by welfare systems, can drive both situational and motivational factors that increase crime. Conversely, the absence of any observed decrease in crime during periods of reduced economic activity challenges theories that assume reduced opportunities automatically lower crime rates.

The GIVAS report reinforces the idea that well-designed social welfare programs act not just as safety nets, but as vital components in crime prevention strategies. It also emphasizes the importance of high-resolution, timely data in identifying early-warning signs of rising crime in economically stressed environments. Policies that anticipate the criminogenic effects of economic crises, through proactive investment in social supports, employment, and education, may mitigate these effects and reduce population-level exposure to victimization.

Additional cross-national research supports the long-term protective role of early social interventions. A CDC-led study analyzing nationally representative data from Malawi, Nigeria, Uganda, and Zambia found that childhood experiences of physical, sexual, or emotional violence significantly increased the likelihood of later violence perpetration among youth aged 13–24 (Swedo et al., 2019). In all four countries, individuals who had experienced multiple forms of childhood violence were up to 20 times more likely to commit acts of violence later in life. The study identified a strong dose–response relationship: the more types of violence experienced in childhood, the higher the odds of perpetration in adolescence or young adulthood. These findings affirm the critical importance of early intervention programs, particularly those that promote family stability, emotional well-being, and trauma-informed services. The authors highlight the relevance of the INSPIRE framework, a technical package developed by the World Health Organization to guide countries in preventing violence against children through coordinated policy and service delivery reforms. In regions where institutional capacity is limited, even basic welfare protections, such as youth counseling, parenting support, and school-based psychosocial resources, can interrupt the intergenerational cycle of violence.

Historical evidence from the United States during the Great Depression further underscores the long-standing protective effects of well-designed welfare programs. Johnson, Kantor, and Fishback (2007, revised 2009) analyzed data across 81 U.S. cities and found that increases in federal relief spending significantly reduced crime, particularly property crime. Specifically, a 20% rise in relief funds led to a 1.4% reduction in overall crime. Both cash and in-kind transfers contributed to this effect by alleviating economic desperation and improving social stability. These findings demonstrate that even during times of national crisis, robust welfare policies can reduce criminal activity by addressing its economic and social roots.

Ultimately, the protective power of welfare lies in its ability to interrupt cycles of marginalization, to lift people out of situations where they are more likely to become either victims or perpetrators of crime. This is not only a matter of economic justice but a foundational strategy in the global fight against crime and victimization.

5.6.4 Fragility and Political Violence in Middle-Income Countries

While victimization is often framed in terms of poverty and deprivation, recent global studies have highlighted that fragility, conflict, and violence (FCV) are increasingly concentrated in middle-income countries. According to a 2022 World Bank report, these countries account for more deaths from political violence and intentional homicides than low-income states. Between 2010 and 2019, middle-income countries experienced over 500,000 fatalities due to political violence, outpacing the toll in poorer nations.

This trend underscores the importance of recognizing how national-level economic growth can mask deep institutional weaknesses. Subnational conflicts, prolonged civil wars, and political violence targeting civilians, including women, are increasingly common in these settings. For example, countries such as Colombia, the Philippines, and Kenya have experienced long-running conflicts rooted in historical exclusion and regional disparities, despite achieving notable economic development milestones.

The report also emphasizes that fragility is not uniformly experienced. In many cases, violence is concentrated in specific geographic regions, often rural or urban peripheries, where state presence is weak and service delivery is minimal. In such areas, development indicators may resemble those of low-income, conflict-affected countries, and communities remain at heightened risk of victimization, both from organized violence and criminal activity.

Additionally, the complexity of violence in middle-income countries is heightened by the presence of overlapping threats such as gang activity, violent extremism, and intercommunal conflict. These interwoven dynamics create "fragile pockets" where traditional crime prevention strategies may be ineffective without broader institutional and peacebuilding reforms.

The implications for crime prevention and victim protection are significant. Interventions that solely target economic inequality or social welfare gaps may fall short if they do not also address the political and institutional dimensions of violence. As the World Bank report concludes, durable solutions require not only targeted social investment but also long-term engagement with FCV drivers through governance reforms, peace processes, and inclusive development planning.

5.6.5 Limitations and Future Research Recommendations

While this chapter provides a comprehensive cross-national examination of socio-economic determinants of victimization, several limitations must be acknowledged. These reflect both the complexity of crime causation and the methodological challenges inherent in comparing data across diverse national contexts.

First, while studies such as Aboya et al. (2022) and Kizilgol & Selim (2017) offer valuable empirical evidence on the relationship between socio-economic variables and crime, their findings also illustrate the context-specific and sometimes contradictory nature of these relationships. For instance, while education was found to have a strong and consistent crime-reducing effect in Pakistan, its effect in India was only significant in the short term. Similarly, unemployment, a commonly cited driver of crime, yielded inconclusive or even counterintuitive results in both studies, suggesting the need for more refined measures of labor market vulnerability, such as informal work, underemployment, or precarious jobs.

Second, both studies rely on macro-level national data, which can obscure important local variations in victimization risk. Urban–rural divides, regional governance differences, and the presence or absence of informal social controls are often flattened in national-level analyses. As such, future research should incorporate micro-level or community-based studies to capture the lived realities of crime and victimization in specific socio-economic settings.

Third, there are persistent challenges in data availability, comparability, and reliability across countries. Differences in legal definitions, crime reporting systems, and institutional capacity can significantly distort international crime statistics. While both studies used robust econometric techniques, their findings are necessarily constrained by the quality and scope of available data. Future studies should continue to develop and utilize standardized, internationally harmonized datasets, particularly in the Global South where crime data remains uneven.

In addition, there is a need for longitudinal research that tracks the long-term effects of education, social welfare, and economic reforms on crime and victimization. Both studies highlighted the importance of short- and long-run dynamics in shaping crime trends, but few datasets or studies follow populations over sufficient time spans to capture these evolving relationships.

Finally, future research should pay closer attention to emerging forms of victimization, such as cybercrime, trafficking, and gender-based violence, particularly in contexts where socio-economic stress intersects with digital and social vulnerabilities. Understanding how poverty, education, and institutional support shape exposure to these crimes will be essential for building comprehensive, forward-looking policy frameworks.

In sum, while the relationship between socio-economic background and victimization is well-supported, it is also highly contingent on local realities, implementation strategies, and evolving social structures. Future research must continue to refine its tools and expand its scope in order to offer meaningful, contextually grounded insights into global patterns of victimization.

5.7 Chapter Summary

This chapter has demonstrated that national socio-economic background is a decisive factor in shaping patterns of victimization across the globe. Drawing on a combination of theoretical frameworks, cross-national comparisons, and empirical case studies, it has shown that poverty, inequality, and limited access to education consistently heighten individuals' vulnerability to crime, both as potential victims and, in some contexts, as offenders.

One of the central insights from this analysis is that economic growth alone does not ensure public safety or reduce victimization. Without equitable distribution of wealth, inclusive education systems, and responsive social institutions, rising GDP may exacerbate disparities that foster criminal behavior and undercut access to justice. Whether in the urban peripheries of Brazil or under-resourced neighborhoods in high-income nations, structural inequality remains a persistent driver of both crime and systemic underprotection.

The empirical studies reviewed throughout this chapter affirm the long-term value of investing in education, income support, and community infrastructure. Social welfare programs, ranging from conditional cash transfers and housing initiatives to early childhood education and trauma-informed youth services, act as crucial buffers against victimization. They do so by addressing not only material deprivation but also the environmental, psychological, and institutional dimensions of crime exposure.

Theoretical perspectives such as Strain Theory and Routine Activity Theory continue to provide important lenses for interpreting these patterns. Strain Theory helps explain how unmet social expectations and resource scarcity can produce frustration that may escalate into criminal behavior. Routine Activity Theory, in turn, clarifies how socio-economic context shapes daily routines, target suitability, and the presence or absence of protective guardianship, especially in areas characterized by under-policing, infrastructure neglect, or digital vulnerability.

Importantly, this chapter has also highlighted the global relevance of these dynamics. From South Asia to Sub-Saharan Africa, from North America to Europe, cross-national evidence points to consistent patterns: where inequality grows, so too do the conditions that facilitate victimization. At the same time, countries that adopt comprehensive and inclusive social policies, such as Scandinavian nations or targeted Latin American interventions, demonstrate that crime prevention is possible when rooted in equity, accountability, and institutional trust.

Ultimately, reducing victimization demands more than reactive policing or punitive policy. It requires a proactive, integrated approach that addresses the root causes of vulnerability. Governments, institutions, and communities must invest in the conditions that allow individuals to live safely, securely, and with dignity. In an era marked by technological transformation, global migration, and deepening social divides, the socio-economic determinants of victimization will remain critical to both research and policy. By placing equity at the center of public safety strategies, societies can move toward more just and resilient futures.

Chapter 6
Cybercrime Victim Services at an International Level

Cybercrime has become a truly global phenomenon, transcending borders and exposing victims to harms that range from financial loss and reputational damage to severe psychological trauma. As such, addressing victimization cannot be confined to national boundaries but requires an understanding of how countries and international organizations have approached cybercrime victim services. This chapter examines the international landscape of victim support, reviewing legal frameworks, national response mechanisms, non-governmental initiatives, and the challenges that persist in providing effective care to victims worldwide.

The discussion begins with international treaties and conventions, such as the Budapest Convention and United Nations initiatives, which establish the legal and cooperative foundations for victim protection. It then considers the role of regional and national systems, including hotlines, compensation programs, and judicial practices that vary widely between developed and developing nations. The chapter also highlights the essential contributions of international NGOs, advocacy groups, and private sector actors, which frequently fill service gaps by offering technical assistance, counseling, or rapid service restoration.

At the same time, the chapter explores systemic challenges that undermine victim support, including cross-border legal barriers, inequalities in resources, low reporting rates, and insufficient integration of victim care into law enforcement practices. Finally, it identifies best practices and policy recommendations emerging from international experience, such as standardized service protocols, collaborative partnerships, and public awareness campaigns, that can inform more resilient, victim-centered frameworks.

By analyzing these diverse approaches, this chapter provides a comparative understanding of the strengths and shortcomings of victim services at the international level. This review not only situates cybercrime victimization within a global context but also lays the groundwork for developing comprehensive, police-facilitated victim service packages in the next chapter.

M. K. A. Lukings et al., *Understanding Cybercrime Victim Services*, Progress in IS,
https://doi.org/10.1007/978-3-032-13273-4_6

6.1 International Legal and Policy Frameworks

The international response to cybercrime victimization has been shaped primarily through global treaties, conventions, and collaborative frameworks. The most significant is the Budapest Convention on Cybercrime, adopted by the Council of Europe in 2001, which remains the only binding international treaty specifically dedicated to cybercrime. It provides a legal framework for international cooperation, harmonization of laws, and mechanisms for cross-border investigations, while also laying the groundwork for the protection of victims' rights [1].

Building on this foundation, the United Nations (UN) has strengthened its role in shaping international cybercrime law. In August 2024, UN member states finalized a new UN Cybercrime Convention, designed to enhance international cooperation, criminalize emerging forms of digital harm, and reinforce safeguards for fundamental rights, including victim protection [2]. In parallel, the International Telecommunication Union (ITU) has developed a Cybercrime Legislation Toolkit to guide countries, particularly developing nations, in drafting legislation that incorporates both effective law enforcement provisions and victim protection mechanisms [3].

At the regional level, multiple frameworks complement these global instruments. The European Union (EU) established the European Cybercrime Centre (EC3) within Europol to coordinate cross-border investigations, provide analytical support, and promote harmonized victim services across member states [4]. The African Union (AU) has participated as an observer in the Budapest Convention process, gradually aligning its policies with international standards to improve both prosecution and victim care [5]. Similarly, the Association of Southeast Asian Nations (ASEAN) has initiated collaborative cybersecurity strategies, focusing on capacity-building, information sharing, and joint training to improve resilience and protection for victims, even though a formal regional convention has yet to be adopted.

International law enforcement organizations also play a critical operational role. Interpol coordinates global cybercrime operations, provides secure data-sharing platforms, and offers training programs to build the capacity of national police forces to support victims effectively [6]. Within Europe, Europol's EC3 works closely with member state police services, offering forensic support, real-time information exchange, and specialized victim-related guidance during large-scale cybercrime investigations [4].

Despite these advances, significant differences remain between developed and developing nations in terms of cybercrime legislation and victim support. In many EU states, comprehensive laws ensure both prosecution of offenders and services for victims, often guided by the Budapest Convention framework [1]. By contrast, many developing countries struggle to enact or enforce such protections due to limited resources, expertise, or political will. To address this disparity, organizations such as the ITU and UNODC provide technical assistance and model laws to strengthen global consistency and ensure that victim rights are not neglected [2, 3].

In summary, while global and regional frameworks have laid strong foundations for addressing cybercrime and protecting victims, the challenge remains in bridging the gap between international norms and national implementation, particularly in resource-constrained jurisdictions.

6.2 National Cybercrime Victim Response Systems

6.2.1 Government-Run Victim Support Services

Government-run victim support services form the backbone of national responses to cybercrime, providing citizens with accessible, trusted, and officially sanctioned pathways for assistance. These services typically include cybercrime hotlines, online reporting portals, national cybersecurity agencies, and compensation programs, each designed to address the multidimensional impacts of cybercrime, from financial harm to psychological trauma.

In the United States, the Internet Crime Complaint Center (IC3) serves as a centralized hub where individuals can report cyber-enabled crimes such as fraud, identity theft, and online harassment. Managed by the FBI in partnership with the National White Collar Crime Center, IC3 not only collects victim complaints but also channels them to the appropriate investigative agencies, offering victims a clear entry point into the law enforcement system [7].

Alongside reporting portals, legal and regulatory frameworks play a key role in supporting victims. The United Nations Office on Drugs and Crime (UNODC) emphasizes that comprehensive cybercrime laws must integrate both prosecutorial powers and victim protection standards, ensuring that national laws address privacy, compensation, and psychological harm [8]. Many governments have adapted such guidance into regulations that require timely responses to incidents, mandate the involvement of service providers, and create legal avenues for restitution.

Specialized initiatives also exist to address the privacy and reputational damages that often accompany cyber victimization. For example, the Cyber Civil Rights Initiative (CCRI) in the U.S. collaborates with government agencies to offer resources, referrals, and a 24/7 helpline for victims of intimate image abuse, addressing both reputational harm and the legal complexities of image-based sexual exploitation [9].

Financial harm remains one of the most pressing impacts of cybercrime. In the U.S., the Office for Victims of Crime (OVC) oversees compensation programs that reimburse eligible victims for certain out-of-pocket expenses linked to cyber-enabled fraud and related crimes [10]. Such compensation initiatives are critical in helping individuals recover from financial loss, particularly in cases where restitution through prosecution is unlikely.

Finally, governments increasingly recognize the psychological impact of cybercrime. Research shows that victims of online fraud and harassment often report heightened levels of anxiety, depression, and in severe cases, suicidal ideation [11]. In response, victim support services increasingly incorporate mental health hotlines, crisis counseling, and referral to trauma-informed therapy, either as part of government programs or in partnership with NGOs.

Taken together, these initiatives demonstrate how government-run services address the full spectrum of victim harm, technical, legal, financial, and emotional. While disparities remain between countries, particularly between resource-rich and resource-limited jurisdictions, such programs illustrate the importance of integrating cybercrime victim services into the broader landscape of national public safety and health policy.

6.2.2 Law Enforcement and Judicial Response

Law enforcement and judicial systems play a central role in both investigating cybercrimes and ensuring that victims receive meaningful support during and after legal proceedings. Effective systems must balance investigative needs with the rights and well-being of victims, integrating legal protections, service restoration, financial remedies, and psychological support.

In the United States, the FBI's Cyber Division has developed advanced capabilities to counter cyber-enabled crimes, including terrorism, ransomware, and financial fraud. These units not only conduct investigations but also engage directly with victims to gather digital evidence, provide case updates, and coordinate recovery efforts [12]. Similarly, the U.S. Secret Service operates Cyber Fraud Task Forces (CFTFs), which unite federal, state, local, and private partners to investigate large-scale fraud and assist in restoring victims' access to compromised services [13].

The importance of robust legal frameworks has been emphasized repeatedly by international organizations. The UNODC highlights that laws must explicitly include victim protections, such as the right to information, compensation, and privacy safeguards, to ensure that investigations do not exacerbate harm [8]. Many jurisdictions have integrated such protections, yet uneven adoption remains a challenge in developing nations.

For many victims, financial compensation is one of the most tangible forms of redress. The Office for Victims of Crime (OVC) administers compensation programs that reimburse victims for financial losses linked to cyber fraud and related offenses. While compensation cannot always cover the full scope of damages, it plays a critical role in stabilizing victims and rebuilding trust in justice systems [10].

Equally important is addressing the psychological impact of cyber victimization during judicial proceedings. Research shows that prolonged investigations and legal delays can deepen victims' distress, sometimes contributing to severe anxiety or suicidal ideation [11]. To mitigate these risks, courts in some jurisdictions have introduced trauma-informed procedures, such as minimizing repeat testimony, providing victim advocates, and ensuring timely updates.

Despite these efforts, many countries still face significant gaps: limited digital forensic expertise, slow case processing times, and insufficient victim participation rights often reduce the effectiveness of judicial responses. Strengthening capacity through training, inter-agency coordination, and international cooperation remains essential to ensuring that victims are not only witnesses in cybercrime cases but also beneficiaries of justice.

6.2.3 Public Awareness and Digital Literacy Programs

Beyond legislation and judicial processes, governments increasingly recognize the importance of public awareness and digital literacy programs as preventative and restorative tools in addressing cybercrime victimization. These initiatives not only help citizens avoid becoming victims but also empower those affected to respond effectively and seek support.

One example is the Cybercrime Support Network (CSN) in the United States, which works with federal agencies, state governments, and corporations to educate individuals and small businesses about cyber threats and victim response strategies. Its platform, *FightCybercrime.org*, provides step-by-step guidance for victims while also serving as a public education hub [14].

Raising legal awareness is also critical. The UNODC has developed resources to educate the public on cyber laws and victim rights, ensuring individuals understand both their protections and obligations under national and international frameworks [8]. Such resources are vital in regions where cyber laws are relatively new or poorly understood.

Privacy protection campaigns have emerged as another important strand. The Cyber Civil Rights Initiative (CCRI) provides advocacy and awareness efforts to combat image-based sexual abuse, offering resources for victims and tools for policymakers to strengthen prevention measures [9]. By framing image abuse as a serious form of victimization, CCRI has raised public consciousness about digital privacy risks.

In parallel, governments have invested in financial literacy programs to mitigate cyber fraud risks. For instance, the Federal Trade Commission (FTC) offers consumer-facing resources to help individuals identify scams, protect personal data, and make informed decisions about online financial interactions [15]. These initiatives are particularly important for vulnerable populations, including seniors and first-time internet users.

Finally, programs addressing the psychological consequences of cybercrime have become more visible. Campaigns led by CSN and its partners emphasize the emotional toll of victimization and normalize seeking help for stress, anxiety, and trauma [14]. By linking technical prevention with mental health support, these initiatives present a more holistic model of public cyber resilience.

Collectively, public awareness and literacy campaigns serve as the first line of defense against cybercrime victimization and as a bridge between individual victims and formal government or NGO-led support structures.

6.3 Cybercrime Victim Assistance Programs and Organizations

6.3.1 International NGOs and Advocacy Groups

In addition to government-led initiatives, a wide range of international non-governmental organizations (NGOs) and advocacy groups provide critical victim services for those affected by cybercrime. These organizations often fill gaps left by national systems, offering specialized expertise, advocacy for victim rights, and cross-border assistance that national agencies may lack.

The CyberPeace Institute, headquartered in Geneva, is one of the most prominent NGOs dedicated to reducing the harm of cyberattacks on vulnerable communities. By collaborating with both governments and private sector partners, the institute provides cybersecurity assistance, incident analysis, and advocacy for stronger victim protection policies, particularly for NGOs and humanitarian organizations at high risk [16].

The Cybercrime Support Network (CSN), a U.S.-based non-profit, assists individuals and small businesses affected by cybercrime. Its platform *FightCybercrime.org* offers practical resources and connects victims with law enforcement, recovery tools, and counseling services. By acting as a trusted intermediary between victims and official authorities, CSN helps lower barriers to reporting and recovery [14].

Another important initiative is The Cyber Helpline, founded in the UK and recently expanded to the U.S. This organization provides free, confidential, expert guidance to individuals experiencing cybercrime and online harms, such as account compromise, stalking, or harassment. Through a volunteer network of security professionals, it delivers both technical advice and emotional support tailored to individual cases [17].

The Cyber Civil Rights Initiative (CCRI) has emerged as a leading advocacy group for victims of image-based sexual abuse. Its services include a 24/7 crisis helpline, legal resources, and policy advocacy aimed at strengthening privacy protections and criminalizing non-consensual image sharing globally. CCRI's work underscores how NGOs can push governments to recognize new forms of digital victimization and embed protections into law [9].

Collectively, these NGOs provide a global safety net for victims, especially in regions where state-led services are limited. They play an essential role in advocating for victim rights, pushing for legislative reform, and ensuring that victims' voices are represented in global cyber policy discussions.

6.3.2 Psychological and Financial Support Services

Cybercrime victimization often leaves individuals facing not only **financial losses** but also significant **psychological trauma**, including anxiety, depression, and, in severe cases, suicidal ideation. Recognizing this dual burden, several international and national programs provide **specialized psychological counseling and financial recovery mechanisms** tailored to cybercrime victims.

The **Financial Crime Resource Center** plays an important role by offering technical assistance to organizations that support fraud and cybercrime victims. It helps victims navigate the complexities of identity theft recovery, fraud remediation, and financial compensation processes, thereby reducing the long-term economic burden of cybercrime [18].

Similarly, the **Office for Victims of Crime (OVC)** in the United States administers funding and grants to expand the capacity of victim service organizations to assist individuals affected by cybercrime. OVC's compensation programs cover eligible expenses such as counseling, lost wages, and financial recovery, ensuring victims have access to both emotional and material forms of support [19].

Psychological support is equally vital. Victims often experience persistent fear, shame, and isolation, particularly in cases of online harassment or fraud-related stigma. Programs like OVC-funded counseling initiatives and crisis hotlines provide trauma-informed mental health services, ensuring that recovery extends beyond financial restitution [19].

Together, these financial and psychological services demonstrate the **need for holistic recovery mechanisms**. While financial compensation alleviates economic damage, psychological support addresses invisible wounds, helping victims regain confidence, restore stability, and reintegrate into digital spaces without lingering fear.

6.3.3 Corporate and Private Sector Involvement

The private sector plays an increasingly important role in supporting cybercrime victims, as many online harms occur on commercial platforms or involve financial institutions. Technology companies, social media providers, and cybersecurity firms are uniquely positioned to offer direct victim support, service restoration, and collaborative prevention programs.

Major technology companies such as Microsoft have actively engaged in global victim assistance initiatives, including partnerships with the CyberPeace Institute. Through these collaborations, Microsoft contributes technical expertise, resources for rapid threat response, and support mechanisms for NGOs and individuals impacted by cybercrime [20].

Private sector involvement also includes direct service restoration. Social media platforms such as Meta and Twitter, as well as service providers like Google, have developed streamlined procedures for recovering compromised accounts, removing abusive content, and improving reporting systems. These measures reduce victims' exposure to further harm and demonstrate the role of corporations as first responders in digital victimization cases [21].

Financial institutions similarly play a critical role in assisting fraud victims. Banks and payment providers increasingly collaborate with law enforcement to detect suspicious activity, freeze fraudulent transactions, and initiate partial reimbursement schemes where possible. Such measures complement government compensation programs by offering immediate financial relief and boosting trust in digital financial systems [22].

Finally, corporations are also beginning to acknowledge the mental health impact of online victimization. By partnering with NGOs and advocacy groups, private companies have supported awareness campaigns and psychological counseling services, particularly for victims of cyber harassment and identity theft [16]. These initiatives highlight how victim care is no longer solely the responsibility of law enforcement but a shared responsibility across the public and private sectors.

In sum, corporate engagement has expanded beyond traditional cybersecurity responsibilities to include victim support as part of corporate social responsibility (CSR). As online services dominate modern life, private sector actors remain indispensable allies in reducing the impact of cybercrime on individuals.

6.4 Challenges and Gaps in Cybercrime Victim Services

6.4.1 Legal and Jurisdictional Barriers

One of the most significant challenges in delivering effective cybercrime victim services lies in the legal and jurisdictional complexities of cross-border cybercrime. Because most cyber offenses involve perpetrators, victims, and infrastructure spanning multiple countries, differences in national legal systems often hinder timely investigation, prosecution, and victim support.

The transnational nature of cybercrime makes victim protection particularly difficult. Victims frequently find themselves caught between multiple jurisdictions, with no single authority responsible for ensuring redress. Studies highlight that inconsistent regulations across borders result in long delays for victims seeking justice and limit law enforcement's ability to secure restitution [23].

Organizations such as Eurojust have emphasized the difficulties caused by fragmented laws, particularly when attempting to prosecute offenders operating across different legal systems. Eurojust reports that inconsistencies in national frameworks impede not only prosecution but also victim services, leading to further harm through prolonged account takeovers, delayed financial recovery, or continued reputational damage [24].

For victims, this often translates into delayed service restoration and limited legal remedies. In cases of online fraud or identity theft, international jurisdictional barriers mean that even when the perpetrator is identified, victims may be left without compensation or closure due to lack of enforceable mechanisms across borders [23].

The psychological impact of these barriers cannot be underestimated. Victims often describe feelings of helplessness, frustration, and emotional exhaustion when faced with long, complex, and uncertain legal processes in foreign jurisdictions [23].

These experiences can compound the trauma of cybercrime itself, highlighting the urgent need for harmonized international victim support protocols.

In sum, legal and jurisdictional barriers undermine the effectiveness of cybercrime victim services, leaving many victims unprotected. Bridging these gaps will require greater alignment of national legal systems, enhanced cross-border agreements, and the adoption of universal minimum standards for victim care.

6.4.2 Resource Inequality

A second critical challenge in cybercrime victim services is the stark resource inequality between high-income and low-income nations. While some countries have established comprehensive legal frameworks, compensation schemes, and psychological support services, others lack even the most basic infrastructure to assist cybercrime victims.

Research highlights that disparities in victim support services are significant: in high-income nations, victims often benefit from specialized cybercrime hotlines, legal aid, and compensation programs, while in low-income regions these services are rare or non-existent [25]. This uneven access leaves millions of victims without formal avenues for redress or recovery.

One key issue is the inadequacy of legal infrastructure. In many developing countries, cybercrime laws remain outdated or insufficiently enforced, which limits victims' rights and the ability to prosecute offenders [25]. Even where legislation exists, under-resourced judicial systems struggle to apply it effectively, leaving victims vulnerable to repeated exploitation.

Financial support mechanisms also reflect this inequality. While developed nations frequently provide compensation through government or NGO-led programs, many low-income countries lack victim compensation schemes altogether, forcing victims to bear financial losses on their own [25].

Access to mental health support is even more uneven. Victims in resource-constrained environments rarely have access to specialized counseling services for cyber trauma. In such contexts, the psychological impacts, stress, anxiety, depression, and stigma, often go unaddressed, compounding the harm of cybercrime [25].

These disparities illustrate how global inequality extends into the digital sphere, reinforcing cycles of victimization and deepening digital divides. Addressing resource inequality will require increased international assistance, capacity-building programs, and cross-border funding mechanisms aimed at ensuring minimum standards of victim protection worldwide.

6.4.3 Low Reporting Rates and Lack of Awareness

Despite the growing prevalence of cybercrime, reporting rates remain alarmingly low, with many victims never contacting law enforcement or support services. This gap stems from a combination of legal, privacy, financial, and psychological barriers that discourage victims from coming forward.

Studies show that a significant number of victims choose not to report incidents due to fear of legal consequences, for example, concerns that admitting to falling for a scam could result in liability or stigma [26]. This is especially relevant in regions with weak consumer protection laws or where victims fear being criminalized for unknowingly engaging with illicit online platforms.

Privacy concerns further deter reporting. Victims often worry that sharing details with authorities will expose sensitive personal information or increase their vulnerability to further harm [27]. In cases such as identity theft, doxxing, or intimate image abuse, victims may view silence as safer than risking public exposure.

Many victims also experience a sense of hopelessness regarding financial recovery. Research indicates that victims who lose money in scams frequently believe that reporting will not lead to reimbursement or prosecution, and thus opt not to engage with authorities [26]. This perception is reinforced in countries where victim compensation programs are absent or poorly publicized.

Finally, the psychological toll of cybercrime contributes to underreporting. Shame, embarrassment, or trauma can prevent victims from seeking help, particularly in sensitive cases such as romance fraud, online sexual exploitation, or harassment [27]. These emotional barriers often silence victims at precisely the moment when support would be most beneficial.

As a result, low reporting rates perpetuate a cycle of invisibility: unreported crimes limit data collection, weaken prevention strategies, and reduce resources for victim services. Breaking this cycle requires public awareness campaigns, confidential reporting mechanisms, and assurance of victim-centered protections that make reporting safe, accessible, and worthwhile.

6.4.4 Limited Integration of Cybercrime Victim Services in law Enforcement

Another major challenge is the limited integration of victim services within law enforcement structures. While many countries have established cybercrime units, these are often designed primarily for investigation and prosecution, with insufficient mechanisms to support the victims themselves.

A key issue is the lack of coordination between police, courts, and victim service organizations. Without integrated protocols, victims may be referred from one agency to another, facing delays and confusion that compound their trauma [28].

For example, gaps in inter-agency cooperation can lead to inefficiencies in prosecution, allowing offenders to continue operating and exposing victims to repeated harm.

Service disruptions are also exacerbated by slow law enforcement responses. In cases of compromised accounts or online fraud, delays in victim assistance can leave individuals without access to essential services for extended periods, furthering both financial and emotional harm [29].

Prolonged legal processes present another challenge. Victims may face years of litigation, during which they often remain vulnerable to harassment, reputational damage, or continuing financial losses. These extended battles can erode trust in justice systems and worsen victims' psychological distress [29].

Ultimately, the failure to integrate victim services into law enforcement frameworks leaves many victims unsupported, reducing reporting rates and undermining public confidence. Addressing this requires institutional reforms, such as embedding victim advocates within cybercrime units, providing training for officers in trauma-informed approaches, and creating rapid-response teams that prioritize both investigation and victim recovery.

6.5 Best Practices and Policy Recommendations

While challenges remain, several best practices and policy recommendations have emerged from international and national experiences in supporting cybercrime victims. These practices highlight the importance of collaboration, standardization, awareness, and cross-sector partnerships in building effective victim services.

Enhancing international collaboration has been a recurring theme. Initiatives such as the European Electronic Crime Task Force (EECTF) demonstrate how shared databases and public-private alliances can improve cross-border cooperation and ensure victims receive timely assistance [30]. Similarly, Interpol has stressed the need for transnational collaboration, noting that cybercrime transcends national borders and requires coordinated responses to protect victims effectively [6].

A second best practice involves the development of standardized victim service protocols. The UNODC emphasizes the importance of harmonizing cybercrime laws to guarantee a minimum level of protection for victims globally [31]. Likewise, the Office for Victims of Crime (OVC) has published best practice guidelines recommending universal standards for victim assistance, including protocols for handling online fraud, identity theft, and cyber harassment [32].

Public education and awareness campaigns also stand out as essential. The National District Attorneys Association (NDAA) guide on elevating victims' voices underscores the importance of legislative advocacy, awareness initiatives, and community education to empower victims and encourage reporting [33]. Complementing this, the Bureau of Justice Statistics (BJS) provides robust data collection and analysis to support evidence-based awareness campaigns and policy-making [34].

Finally, public-private partnerships (PPPs) have proven effective in extending the reach and capacity of victim services. The UNODC has highlighted how PPPs strengthen victim support mechanisms by leveraging the resources of governments, NGOs, and corporations [31]. Similarly, the World Economic Forum (WEF) stresses the value of collaborative frameworks to disrupt cybercrime networks and deliver victim-centered solutions at scale [35].

In conclusion, best practices emphasize that no single entity can fully address the needs of cybercrime victims. Only through international cooperation, standardization, education, and partnerships can nations build sustainable and resilient systems that place victims at the center of cybercrime responses.

6.6 Chapter Summary

This chapter has examined the evolving landscape of cybercrime victim services at the international level, highlighting both the achievements and persistent gaps across legal, institutional, and community frameworks. A review of international treaties and conventions, such as the Budapest Convention, revealed how multilateral instruments have laid the groundwork for cooperation while underscoring the challenges of ensuring consistent victim protections across borders. National response systems, from government-run hotlines and compensation programs to judicial and law enforcement mechanisms, further illustrate the diverse ways countries attempt to support victims, though with varying levels of effectiveness.

The role of non-governmental organizations and advocacy groups emerged as critical, particularly in filling gaps where governments have limited resources or where victims require specialized assistance such as trauma counseling or advocacy for privacy rights. Meanwhile, the private sector has increasingly assumed responsibility in areas such as service restoration, financial reimbursement, and awareness campaigns, reflecting a broader recognition that cybercrime victim care is a shared responsibility.

At the same time, the chapter has identified significant challenges and gaps: cross-border legal barriers, resource inequalities, low reporting rates, and limited integration of victim services within law enforcement. These issues highlight the fragility of current frameworks and the pressing need for greater harmonization, capacity building, and victim-centered reforms.

Drawing on best practices, such as international cooperation mechanisms, standardized victim service protocols, public education, and public-private partnerships, this review makes clear that effective victim support requires multilayered collaboration. Victims are best served when legal, financial, psychological, and technical support converge into a holistic system.

This international analysis sets the stage for Chap. 7, which builds on these insights to propose a Comprehensive Cybercrime Victim Service Package tailored for law enforcement agencies. By integrating lessons learned from global practices and adapting them to local contexts, Chap. 7 will outline how police and national authorities can move beyond prevention and prosecution to offer victims the direct, immediate, and holistic support they need [8, 10, 11].

References

1. Council of Europe. (2001). *Convention on cybercrime* (Budapest convention). https://www.coe.int/cybercrime.
2. United Nations Office on Drugs and Crime (UNODC). (2024). *UN Cybercrime Convention.* https://www.unodc.org
3. International Telecommunication Union. (2021). *Toolkit for cybercrime legislation.* ITU.
4. Europol. (2023). *European Cybercrime Centre (EC3).* https://www.europol.europa.eu
5. Council of Europe. (2022). *Cybercrime convention committee: African union observer role.* https://www.coe.int/cybercrime.
6. Interpol. (2023). *Cybercrime Directorate–Victim Support & Cooperation.* https://www.interpol.int
7. Internet Crime Complaint Center (IC3). (2023). *2022 internet crime report.* Federal Bureau of Investigation. https://www.ic3.gov
8. United Nations Office on Drugs and Crime (UNODC). (2022). *Comprehensive study on cybercrime: Legal frameworks and victim protection.* https://www.unodc.org
9. Cyber Civil Rights Initiative (CCRI). (2023). *24/7 Helpline for victims of non-consensual image abuse.* https://www.cybercivilrights.org
10. Office for Victims of Crime (OVC). (2023). *Victim compensation programs.* U.S. Department of Justice. https://ovc.ojp.gov
11. The Guardian. (2022). *Cybercrime's hidden toll: The psychological impact on victims.* The Guardian. https://www.theguardian.com
12. Office of Justice Programs. (2022). *FBI Cyber Division–Investigating and preventing cybercrime.* U.S. Department of Justice. https://www.justice.gov
13. United States Secret Service. (2023). *Cyber Fraud Task Forces (CFTFs).* U.S. Department of Homeland Security. https://www.secretservice.gov
14. Cybercrime Support Network (CSN). (2023). *FightCybercrime.org—Resources for individuals and small businesses.* https://fightcybercrime.org
15. Federal Trade Commission (FTC). (2023). *Consumer advice on avoiding online scams.* https://www.ftc.gov
16. CyberPeace Institute. (2023). *Reducing the harm of cyberattacks on vulnerable communities.* Geneva. https://cyberpeaceinstitute.org.
17. The Cyber Helpline. (2023). *Free expert help for victims of cybercrime and online harm.* https://www.thecyberhelpline.com
18. Financial Crime Resource Center. (2022). *Supporting organizations that assist fraud and cybercrime victims.* Victims of Crime. https://victimsofcrime.org
19. Office for Victims of Crime (OVC). (2023). *Victim assistance and compensation programs.* U.S. Department of Justice. https://ovc.ojp.gov
20. Microsoft News. (2023). *Microsoft's partnerships to support cybercrime victims.* https://news.microsoft.com
21. CyberPeace Institute. (2023). *Collaborations with private sector to enhance victim resilience.* Geneva. https://cyberpeaceinstitute.org
22. World Economic Forum. (2022). *Financial institutions and cyber resilience: Protecting fraud victims.* WEF. https://www.weforum.org
23. International Journal of Research and Development Organization (IJRDO). (2022). *Cross-border challenges in prosecuting cybercrime and protecting victims.* IJRDO. https://www.ijrdo.org

24. Eurojust. (2022). *Judicial cooperation in cross-border cybercrime cases.* European Union Agency for Criminal Justice Cooperation. https://www.eurojust.europa.eu
25. Law Enforcement Bulletin (LEB). (2022). *Challenges of cybercrime victim support in resource-limited settings.* Federal Bureau of Investigation. https://leb.fbi.gov
26. MDPI. (2022). Barriers to reporting cybercrime: Legal and psychological perspectives. *Journal of Cybersecurity and Privacy, 2*(4), 215–229.
27. MDPI. (2023). Victim perspectives on privacy risks and underreporting of cybercrime. *Journal of Cybersecurity and Privacy, 3*(2), 101–118.
28. Law Enforcement Bulletin (LEB). (2022). *Coordination challenges in cybercrime investigations and victim support.* Federal Bureau of Investigation. https://leb.fbi.gov
29. Law Enforcement Bulletin (LEB). (2023). *Delays in prosecution and service restoration in cybercrime cases.* Federal Bureau of Investigation. https://leb.fbi.gov
30. Wikipedia. (2022). *European Electronic Crime Task Force (EECTF).* https://en.wikipedia.org/wiki/European_Electronic_Crime_Task_Force
31. United Nations Office on Drugs and Crime (UNODC). (2022). *Public-private partnerships on cybercrime and victim protection.* https://www.unodc.org
32. Office for Victims of Crime (OVC). (2022). *Best practices guidelines: Crime victim services.* U.S. Department of Justice. https://ovc.ojp.gov
33. National District Attorneys Association (NDAA). (2022). *Elevating victims' voices at a critical time.* NDAA Publications. https://ndaa.org
34. Bureau of Justice Statistics (BJS). (2023). *Victim Services Statistical Research Program (VSSRP).* U.S. Department of Justice. https://bjs.ojp.gov
35. World Economic Forum (WEF). (2022). *Disrupting cybercrime networks: A collaboration framework.* https://www.weforum.org

Chapter 7
Cybercrime Prevention Techniques & Comprehensive Cyber Crime Victim Service Package Proposal

7.1 Introduction: Toward a Victim-Centered Cybercrime Response

The widespread adoption of digital technologies has significantly expanded the reach and impact of cybercrime. As highlighted in earlier chapters, cybercrime is no longer limited to financial institutions or corporate environments; individuals are now frequently targeted, often lacking the knowledge, tools, or support needed to respond effectively. Chapter 2 detailed the nature and categories of cybercrime, while Chap. 3 profiled typical victims, many of whom are vulnerable, digitally unprepared, and unaware of where to seek help. Chapter 4 then examined the profound emotional, financial, and social impacts these crimes have on victims, emphasizing the urgency of developing comprehensive and accessible support systems.

Chapter 5 provided a comparative analysis of legal frameworks and support services in countries such as Australia, Finland, the United Kingdom, and Canada. These case studies demonstrate that while many jurisdictions have established reporting portals or technical hotlines, few offer a fully integrated, police-connected support model tailored to the individual cybercrime victim. Programs like Australia's IDCARE, the UK's Action Fraud, and Finland's multi-agency victim coordination model offer promising practices that inform this chapter's proposed solution.

Also, Chap. 6 highlighted international frameworks such as the Budapest Convention, UN cybercrime initiatives, and regional models in the EU, ASEAN, and Africa. It also reviewed national reporting systems like the FBI's IC3 and NGO-led programs such as the Cyber Helpline and CyberPeace Institute. These insights form the basis for the proposed comprehensive package, demonstrating how fragmented global practices can be synthesized into a unified, police-facilitated model.

Building on this foundation, Chap. 7 introduces a Comprehensive Cybercrime Victim Services Package intended for use by national or regional law enforcement agencies, such as the Royal Police. The goal is to enable first responders to provide more than just investigative follow-up: they must be equipped to stabilize, guide, and

M. K. A. Lukings et al., *Understanding Cybercrime Victim Services*, Progress in IS,
https://doi.org/10.1007/978-3-032-13273-4_7

connect victims to the broader ecosystem of support. This includes not only technical advice but also legal aid referrals, psychological first aid, identity recovery tools, and long-term case management [1, 2].

Unlike prevention-focused models aimed at organizational risk mitigation, this package is designed to serve individual members of the public, anyone who calls the police after experiencing a cyber incident such as fraud, harassment, sextortion, identity theft, or ransomware. The aim is to ensure that every report receives a compassionate, informed, and structured response, minimizing harm and empowering victims to recover with dignity and confidence [3, 4].

The following sections will outline the principles, categories, design components, and implementation framework of this proposed service package, anchored in both international practice and the analytical findings of the previous chapters.

7.2 Principles of Victim-Centered Police Response

When individuals experience cybercrime, whether in the form of identity theft, online harassment, romance fraud, sextortion, or digital stalking, their first instinct is often to turn to law enforcement. Yet, as detailed in Chap. 4, many victims encounter skepticism, limited assistance, or a lack of follow-up from authorities. This disconnect not only delays recovery but can also intensify the emotional and psychological trauma caused by the crime.

To bridge this gap, a shift toward victim-centered policing in cybercrime contexts is essential. This section presents the core principles that should guide the design and delivery of police-based cybercrime victim services. These principles draw directly from the victim profiles and emotional impacts outlined in Chap. 4, as well as international examples of service delivery models examined in Chap. 5, including Australia's IDCARE and the UK's Action Fraud initiative [1–5].

1. Trauma-Informed and Survivor-Sensitive Policing

Cybercrime often produces emotional harm comparable to, or in some cases exceeding, that of traditional crimes. Victims may feel violated, exposed, or manipulated, particularly in cases involving social engineering, blackmail, or non-consensual image distribution. A trauma-informed approach requires officers to:

- Avoid victim-blaming or dismissive attitudes.
- Recognize the possibility of shame, guilt, and fear during disclosure.
- Respond with empathy, patience, and validation, especially during initial contact.

This approach aligns with best practices used in domestic violence and sexual assault response, as well as with victim assistance strategies implemented in Australia and Finland (Chap. 5).

2. **Recognizing Digital Harm as Real Harm**

A key barrier to effective victim support is the outdated perception that digital crimes are less serious than physical ones. However, as documented in Chap. 4, victims of cyber harassment, deepfake abuse, and financial fraud report tangible consequences, including mental health deterioration, job loss, and family disruption. Victim-centered policing acknowledges that:

- Emotional and reputational damage in cyberspace can have long-term real-world effects.
- The invisibility of the crime scene does not lessen the severity of the offense.
- Police must treat cybercrime complaints with the same urgency as physical assaults, especially when a victim is in acute distress.

3. **Minimizing Secondary Victimization**

Secondary victimization occurs when the response to a victim's complaint causes additional harm, often through disbelief, bureaucratic delays, or exposure to public scrutiny. To avoid this, officers must:

- Provide clear explanations of what victims can expect during and after the reporting process.
- Offer multiple reporting options (in person, phone, online, anonymous).
- Avoid overwhelming the victim with technical jargon or unrealistic expectations.
- Ensure timely referrals to specialized services for further support.

As described in Chap. 5, models like the UK's centralized Action Fraud reporting system and Finland's interagency coordination hub are structured to minimize fragmentation and ensure victims are not left navigating the system alone.

4. **Equity, Accessibility, and Cultural Sensitivity**

Victim-centered response must be inclusive and adaptable to a range of lived experiences. Victims may be:

- Elderly individuals unfamiliar with digital platforms.
- Youth affected by cyberbullying or sextortion.
- Newcomers or non-native speakers unsure how to report or navigate the system.

Service design must reflect this diversity by incorporating multilingual options, culturally sensitive protocols, and accessible tools for victims with disabilities. These considerations are integral to trauma-informed models and are reflected in service delivery approaches in Canada and Australia (Chap. 5).

Together, these principles provide a foundation for the structured services proposed in the following sections. They ensure that the Royal Police, or any national law enforcement agency adopting this model, can transition from a reactive investigative posture to a **supportive, trusted, and holistic first response system** for cybercrime victims.

7.3 Classification of Police-Facilitated Victim Services

Building on the victim-centered principles outlined in the previous section, this part of the chapter introduces a structured classification of services that law enforcement officers, particularly frontline responders and dispatch units, can provide or coordinate when engaging with victims of cybercrime. These services are not intended to replace investigations, but to complement them by ensuring that victims receive immediate care, harm reduction, information, and access to long-term recovery resources [2, 3].

As documented in Chaps. 4 and 5, many victims disengage or suffer prolonged harm not due to the cyber incident itself, but due to a lack of clear, accessible, and timely support after reporting. International programs such as Australia's IDCARE, Canada's RCMP victim services, and the UK's Action Fraud portal demonstrate the importance of segmenting support into categories that are easy to operationalize at the police level [1, 4, 5].

The framework for classification in this section is informed by Chap. 6's review of existing models, such as government-operated hotlines and reporting portals (e.g., the U.S. IC3), law enforcement task forces like the U.S. Secret Service's Cyber Fraud units, and NGO-based assistance programs including the Cyber Helpline. Collectively, these examples demonstrate how victim services can be translated into distinct yet interconnected categories of support.

Building on these models, this section organizes the functions into five operational service categories, each targeting a specific dimension of victim need at the point of police contact. This structured approach enables law enforcement to standardize protocols, allocate resources effectively, and guide victims through the recovery process with greater assurance and consistency.

7.3.1 Digital Containment & Technical Harm Reduction

When individuals report a cybercrime, whether involving fraud, account compromise, sextortion, or malicious communications, they are often still in the midst of the incident or unsure whether the threat has ended. As identified in Chap. 4, this uncertainty leads to fear, confusion, and inaction. Law enforcement responders, even without technical expertise, can play a crucial role in helping victims take basic containment measures to stop further harm and begin the process of recovery.

This category focuses on low-risk, evidence-preserving, and immediately actionable guidance that police officers or trained victim services personnel can offer. These actions are designed to reduce panic, empower the victim, and maintain the integrity of digital evidence.

Key Actions:

- Basic Containment Advice

  Officers can guide the victim to:

○ Disconnect from Wi-Fi or mobile data to prevent further unauthorized access.
○ Cease communication with the suspected attacker (e.g., romance fraud, blackmail).
○ Log out of sessions where appropriate.

- Evidence Preservation Instructions

  Victims are encouraged not to delete suspicious messages, emails, or images. Officers can suggest:

  ○ Taking screenshots of communications and profiles.
  ○ Saving timestamps, account handles, and transaction records.
  ○ Storing physical devices securely if they may later require analysis.

- Password & Account Recovery Tips

  Victims can be directed to:

  ○ Immediately change passwords on critical accounts (e.g., email, banking, social media).
  ○ Enable multi-factor authentication (MFA) where possible.
  ○ Avoid using the same device if compromise is suspected.

- Referral to Trusted Technical Support Channels

  Rather than diagnosing devices or installing tools, officers should offer a printed or digital resource list of verified, non-commercial cybersecurity support services. These may include:

  ○ National or provincial cyber support centers.
  ○ University-operated helplines.
  ○ Government-approved volunteer tech response groups.

This approach reflects best practices from Australia's IDCARE Response Plan, which equips non-technical staff with structured scripts to deliver meaningful containment advice. It emphasizes public safety, non-intrusion, and clarity, while ensuring that police remain within the boundaries of legal and technical responsibility.

7.3.2 Psychosocial First Aid

Victims of cybercrime frequently suffer emotional and psychological consequences in addition to financial or reputational harm. As shown in Chap. 4, victims of harassment, sextortion, impersonation, and online threats often experience fear, shame, panic, and in severe cases, trauma or suicidal thoughts. Law enforcement officers, as first responders, must be prepared to offer basic emotional stabilization and ensure rapid referral to professional help.

This service category, psychosocial first aid, does not involve counseling or diagnosis. Instead, it focuses on trauma-sensitive support and triage, enabling the officer to de-escalate distress and guide the victim toward recovery resources.

Key Actions:

- Active Listening and Reassurance: Officers use nonjudgmental, empathetic language to acknowledge the harm, validate emotions, and reduce panic. A calm, supportive tone can immediately re-establish a sense of safety.
- Emotional Stabilization Techniques: In visibly distressed individuals, officers can encourage grounding steps (e.g., slow breathing) and ensure the victim is not alone. In urgent cases, officers should engage 24/7 mental health crisis lines or mobile support units.
- Provision of Mental Health Resources: Victims receive a printed or digital handout listing national and local mental health services, hotlines, and support centers, tailored by demographic (e.g., youth, women, elderly, immigrants).
- Consent-Based Referral to Trauma Support: With the victim's agreement, officers can trigger referrals to certified social workers, crisis counselors, or community-based trauma services (e.g., programs for cyberbullying or gender-based digital violence).

By offering immediate, compassionate support and facilitating access to specialized care, this service ensures that police engagement becomes a pathway to recovery, not a source of further fear, frustration, or dismissal.

7.3.3 Legal Guidance & Navigation

For many victims of cybercrime, the legal system can appear opaque, fragmented, or intimidating. As discussed in Chap. 5, national frameworks often lack clearly defined processes for reporting, prosecuting, or resolving cyber incidents, particularly those involving cross-jurisdictional elements, digital impersonation, or emotional harm. Victims frequently feel lost after making a report, unsure of their rights, options, or next steps. This service category addresses that gap by equipping law enforcement officers and victim service personnel to provide clear, accessible legal orientation and guidance.

The objective is not to offer legal advice or representation, but to ensure that victims:

- Understand their basic rights.
- Are informed about what the police can and cannot do.
- Know how to access further legal assistance.

Key Actions:

- Explanation of Legal Protections and Jurisdictional Scope: Officers briefly clarify whether the victim's case falls under criminal law, civil law, or online platform terms of service. This includes explaining which elements police can investigate and which may fall outside their mandate.

- Guidance on Documentation and Evidence Standards: Victims are instructed on what to document (e.g., dates, communications, screenshots, transaction IDs) and how to preserve it for potential legal processes.
- Referral to Legal Aid or Rights Advocacy Services: With the victim's consent, police can refer them to:
  - Legal aid clinics.
  - Digital rights organizations.
  - Specialized services for vulnerable groups (e.g., survivors of sextortion or defamation).
- Assistance with Filing or Advancing Reports: Officers may assist the victim in:
  - Submitting detailed reports to cybercrime units or prosecutors.
  - Contacting data protection authorities or ombudspersons where appropriate.
  - Understanding the follow-up timeline and how to check case status.
- Connection to Platform-Level Reporting and Takedown Services: For crimes involving social media, impersonation, or image abuse, victims are guided on how to report content directly to platforms, using official portals or law enforcement liaison contacts when available.

This support model draws on practices used in the UK's Action Fraud victim portal and the legal triage layer offered by Canada's public defenders and victim services. The focus is on transparency, empowerment, and access, reducing legal confusion and ensuring victims are not left alone to navigate complex systems.

7.3.4 Financial & Identity Protection Services

One of the most disruptive consequences of cybercrime for individual victims is the compromise of their financial accounts, personal identity, or digital reputation. As highlighted in Chap. 4, incidents involving phishing, social engineering, banking fraud, and identity theft often result in immediate financial loss, prolonged administrative burden, and serious emotional stress. Yet, many victims are unaware of how to respond effectively, or whether they should involve banks, credit bureaus, or government agencies.

This service category enables law enforcement to assist victims in taking urgent, protective actions to limit financial damage and begin identity restoration. Officers are not expected to act as financial advisors, but rather to provide guided triage, clear referrals, and standardized tools to help victims secure their personal and financial information.

Key Actions:

- Encouraging Rapid Contact with Financial Institutions: Victims are advised to immediately notify their bank(s), credit card provider(s), or payment platforms to:
    - o Flag suspicious transactions.
    - o Freeze or close compromised accounts.
    - o Initiate fraud investigation processes.
- Referral to Credit Protection Services: Victims are informed about their right to:
    - o Request credit freezes or fraud alerts through national credit bureaus.
    - o Access identity theft recovery tools (e.g., Equifax/TransUnion in Canada).
    - o Use fraud monitoring services if provided by banks or public agencies.
- Provision of Identity Recovery Checklists: Officers can provide a structured checklist tailored to the type of breach, including:
    - o Reporting stolen SIN/SSNs or government ID numbers.
    - o Resetting linked email or social accounts.
    - o Updating breached security questions or personal info.
- Support in Filing Fraud Affidavits or Reports: If victims require formal documentation for banks or insurance, officers can assist in generating police reports or victim declarations where applicable.
- Referral to National Victim Support Hotlines: Victims can be directed to services such as Australia's IDCARE, Canada's Canadian Anti-Fraud Centre (CAFC), or other public helplines for ongoing identity protection assistance.

These services protect victims from continued exploitation, ensure timely financial remediation, and restore a sense of control. By integrating this into the police response workflow, the model ensures that victims are not left alone to navigate a complex web of financial recovery protocols.

7.3.5 Education, Empowerment & Follow-up

While containment, support, and recovery are essential in the immediate aftermath of a cybercrime, sustainable victim resilience depends on longer-term empowerment and connection to reliable resources. As illustrated in Chap. 4, many victims are left in a vulnerable state, uncertain how to protect themselves going forward and hesitant to re-engage with digital spaces. Without proactive follow-up and practical education, they may become repeat targets or disengage entirely from online services, exacerbating digital exclusion and emotional distress.

This service category ensures that law enforcement and affiliated agencies support victims beyond the initial incident by offering structured educational tools, ongoing touchpoints, and guided pathways to digital recovery and confidence-building.

Key Actions:

- Delivery of a Victim Resource Package: At the time of first contact or shortly after, victims should receive a printed or digital guide that includes:
    - o Practical tips for digital self-protection.
    - o Lists of trustworthy cybersecurity tools and hotlines.
    - o Platform-specific reporting links and fraud alert mechanisms.
    - o Contact information for further support (mental health, financial, legal).
- Educational Content Tailored by Demographic: Materials should be curated based on the victim's age, background, and digital literacy. For instance:
    - o Seniors may benefit from simplified visual instructions.
    - o Youth may be directed to mobile-friendly content and peer-led awareness platforms.
    - o Immigrants may need translated guides or culturally relevant examples.
- Optional Referral to Public Training Programs: Victims can be directed to free, non-commercial workshops or e-learning programs (e.g., government-sponsored digital literacy campaigns or nonprofit-run cyber hygiene training).
- Scheduled Follow-Up by Victim Support Units: When appropriate and with consent, police or victim services may follow up:
    - o To check on recovery progress.
    - o To provide updates on legal or investigative actions.
    - o To re-engage victims with support programs if needed.
- Feedback Collection for Service Improvement
    - o Victims can be invited to anonymously share their experience through a survey or feedback tool, helping agencies refine services and ensure accountability.

This final category ensures that the police response is not only reactive but transformative, supporting the victim in regaining digital agency, trust, and resilience. It mirrors the sustained engagement model used in Finland's multi-agency victim care programs and Canada's RCMP-led community outreach efforts [3–5].

The five categories outlined in this section provide a clear operational framework for police to deliver structured, compassionate, and effective support to cybercrime victims. By addressing immediate harm, emotional stabilization, legal orientation, financial protection, and long-term empowerment, this model ensures that victims receive holistic assistance from the moment they reach out for help. Grounded in the findings from earlier chapters and informed by proven practices in countries such as Australia, the UK, and Finland, this classification positions law enforcement not only as investigators but as active partners in a victim's recovery journey.

7.4 The Comprehensive Victim Services Package: Components & Design

The classification of police-facilitated victim services outlined in Sect. 7.3 provides the conceptual framework for a structured, law enforcement–driven response to cybercrime victimization. This section translates that framework into a practical, deployable package that can be adopted by agencies such as the Royal Police and adapted for regional or national use.

The proposed package is designed to be modular, allowing agencies to implement it in stages or scale it according to resources, while maintaining a consistent, victim-centered approach across all points of contact. Drawing on best practices identified in Chap. 5, including Australia's IDCARE model, the UK's Action Fraud system, and Canada's RCMP victim services structure, the package integrates technical guidance, emotional support, legal navigation, financial safeguards, and empowerment tools into a cohesive, easy-to-use set of resources and protocols [1–5].

In addition, the framework builds on international lessons highlighted in Chap. 6, such as Europol's EC3 coordination model, the U.S. Office for Victims of Crime compensation schemes, and NGO initiatives like the CyberPeace Institute and the Cyber Helpline. These examples illustrate how fragmented practices can be consolidated into a comprehensive, police-facilitated victim services package that provides integrated, reliable, and accessible support. Each component described in the following subsections is designed for direct use by frontline officers, dispatch units, and victim services staff, ensuring that every victim, regardless of their digital literacy, background, or location, receives the same standard of care and assistance.

7.4.1 Component 1: First-Responder Toolkit

The First-Responder Toolkit is the foundation of the comprehensive victim services package. It equips frontline police officers, call handlers, and victim service staff with standardized, easy-to-follow resources that enable a consistent and effective response to any cybercrime report. As established in Sect. 7.3 and supported by international models such as Australia's IDCARE Response Plans and Canada's RCMP Victim Services protocols, a standardized toolkit ensures victims receive timely, accurate, and supportive guidance from their first point of contact.

Key Elements of the Toolkit:

- **Incident Assessment Script**

  A step-by-step question guide for officers or dispatch staff to quickly determine:

  - o Type of cybercrime (fraud, harassment, identity theft, sextortion, hacking, etc.).
  - o Urgency level (ongoing harm vs. post-incident reporting).

○ Immediate safety or containment needs.

- **Digital Containment Quick Guide**

  A one-page checklist for non-technical responders, covering:

  ○ Disconnecting devices from networks.
  ○ Preserving evidence (screenshots, logs, emails).
  ○ Avoiding further engagement with the attacker.

- **Evidence Preservation Template**

  Simple forms for recording incident details, including:

  ○ Timeline of events.
  ○ Known attacker identifiers (usernames, phone numbers, email addresses).
  ○ Screenshots or copies of communications.

- **Referral Pathway Map**

  A visual diagram showing where to direct victims for:

  ○ Legal aid.
  ○ Mental health support.
  ○ Financial and identity protection services.
  ○ Platform-level content takedowns.

- **Communication Guidelines**

  ○ Brief instructions on trauma-informed language, avoiding jargon, and maintaining victim trust.

By placing these tools directly in the hands of first responders, whether in printed form, mobile app format, or integrated into dispatch software, police can ensure that every interaction is consistent, professional, and supportive, regardless of the responder's technical background.

7.4.2 Component 2: Victim Information Packet

The Victim Information Packet is a ready-to-distribute resource provided to every individual who reports a cybercrime, either in person, by phone, or online. Its purpose is to give victims clear, concise, and actionable information immediately after first contact, reducing confusion, promoting informed decision-making, and helping prevent further harm. As demonstrated in the UK's Action Fraud victim resources and Finland's multi-agency victim care guides, early access to plain-language, structured information significantly improves recovery outcomes.

Key Elements of the Packet:

- **Plain-Language Explanation of the Crime Type**

A brief description of the reported cybercrime category, its common impacts, and potential next steps, avoiding technical jargon.

- **Immediate Safety and Containment Steps**

  Customized advice for the specific incident type (e.g., enabling MFA, freezing bank accounts, blocking contacts, reporting to platforms).

- **Victim Rights and Reporting Process**

  An outline of:

  - What the police can and cannot do under current laws.
  - How evidence will be handled and stored.
  - Expected timelines for updates.

- **Contact List for Support Services**

  Verified local and national contacts for:

  - Mental health and crisis counseling.
  - Legal assistance and advocacy.
  - Financial and identity protection services.
  - Technical help from trusted non-commercial providers.

- **Step-by-Step Self-Recovery Checklist**

  Actions victims can take immediately, within 48 hours, and in the longer term, tailored by incident type.

- **Feedback and Follow-Up Information**

  Instructions on how victims can request updates, submit additional evidence, or provide feedback on the service received.

The Victim Information Packet can be delivered in multiple formats:

- Printed booklet for in-person reports.
- Downloadable PDF sent via secure email.
- Web or mobile-friendly version linked from the police cybercrime reporting portal.

By giving victims clear, credible, and accessible information from the outset, the police ensure that survivors are empowered participants in their own recovery, not passive recipients of an opaque process.

7.4.3 Component 3: Referral and Escalation Map

The Referral and Escalation Map is a structured guide that enables police officers, call handlers, and victim service staff to quickly connect victims with the most appropriate support services, while ensuring that complex or high-risk cases are escalated to specialized units without delay. As noted in Chap. 5, one of the key shortcomings in existing systems is the lack of a clear pathway from first contact to specialized help, which can leave victims feeling abandoned or forced to navigate a confusing web of agencies on their own.

Drawing on the multi-agency coordination model used in Finland and the tiered case management approach of Australia's IDCARE, this map ensures every victim receives timely, coordinated, and needs-specific support.

Key Elements of the Referral and Escalation Map:

- **Service Pathway Diagram**

  A visual flowchart that guides responders through:

  - Determining the urgency of the case.
  - Identifying the relevant type of assistance (technical, legal, mental health, financial).
  - Directing the victim to vetted service providers.

- **Specialized Escalation Triggers**

  Criteria that require immediate escalation to cybercrime investigation units, such as:

  - Ongoing threats to life or safety.
  - Child exploitation material or grooming.
  - High-value financial theft or fraud affecting multiple victims.
  - Coordinated harassment campaigns.

- **Partner Agency Contact Directory**

  Up-to-date contact information for:

  - National hotlines (e.g., Canadian Anti-Fraud Centre).
  - Nonprofit victim advocacy organizations.
  - Government data protection authorities.
  - Crisis counseling and mental health providers.

- **Platform Liaison Contacts**

  Designated escalation points for urgent takedown requests with major social media, messaging, and content-hosting platforms.

- **Multi-Language and Accessibility Options**

  Referral materials available in multiple languages and formats (including large print and easy-read versions) to ensure equitable access.

By integrating the Referral and Escalation Map into both printed toolkits and digital police systems, officers can deliver swift, coordinated, and appropriate connections to the broader victim support network, reducing delays and preventing victims from having to repeat their story multiple times to different agencies.

7.4.4 Component 4: Case Management Dashboard

The Case Management Dashboard is a secure, centralized system that enables law enforcement and victim service teams to track each cybercrime victim's case from first contact through resolution and follow-up. As highlighted in Chap. 5, one of the most common victim frustrations is the lack of updates or visibility into the status of their report. Without a structured tracking system, victims may disengage, lose trust in law enforcement, or miss important deadlines for legal, financial, or technical recovery.

Inspired by Canada's RCMP case tracking for victim services and Australia's IDCARE client management system, this dashboard is designed to integrate into existing police IT platforms while respecting privacy and confidentiality requirements.

Key Elements of the Dashboard:

- **Case Intake Record**

  Captures all initial report details, including:

  - Type of incident.
  - Incident timeline.
  - Evidence provided.
  - Immediate actions taken.

- **Victim Support Plan**

  A personalized action plan based on the five service categories outlined in Sect. 7.3 (technical harm reduction, psychosocial support, legal guidance, financial/identity protection, and empowerment/follow-up).

- **Task and Referral Tracking**

  Logs when and where the victim was referred (e.g., legal aid, crisis counseling, financial services) and records any confirmation of service delivery.

- **Status Updates and Notifications**

  Allows victim service officers to record progress notes and, where appropriate, automatically send secure updates to victims regarding:

  - Investigative steps.
  - Platform takedown status.
  - Follow-up appointments.

- **Multi-Agency Access (Controlled)**

  Enables authorized partner agencies (e.g., mental health services, victim advocacy organizations) to update relevant portions of the case file, ensuring better coordination and reduced duplication.

- **Privacy and Consent Management**

  Built-in safeguards to ensure that victim data is handled in compliance with privacy laws (e.g., GDPR, PIPEDA) and only shared with consent.

By implementing a Case Management Dashboard, law enforcement agencies can provide victims with transparent, coordinated, and accountable support, transforming the reporting process into an ongoing partnership rather than a one-time transaction.

7.4.5 Component 5: Community Outreach and Awareness Resources

Cybercrime victim support is most effective when prevention and awareness are embedded into community engagement. While the primary focus of the Comprehensive Victim Services Package is on responding to incidents, proactive outreach helps reduce victimization rates, empowers at-risk groups, and strengthens trust between law enforcement and the public. As discussed in Chap. 4, lack of awareness is a major contributor to both the likelihood of becoming a victim and the underreporting of incidents.

This component draws on the community engagement strategies used by Canada's RCMP Cybercrime Awareness Campaign and the public education model embedded in Australia's IDCARE service, adapting them for deployment by local and national police services.

Key Elements of Community Outreach and Awareness Resources:

- **Educational Campaign Toolkits**

  Ready-to-use materials (posters, infographics, social media posts, radio scripts) addressing common scams, digital hygiene tips, and safe online behavior. These can be adapted for local community needs.

- **Targeted Outreach for Vulnerable Groups**

  Customized resources for:

  - Seniors at risk of tech-support and investment scams.
  - Youth targeted by sextortion, cyberbullying, and grooming.
  - Immigrant communities facing language and cultural barriers in reporting cybercrime.

- **Public Workshops and Webinars**

  Law enforcement-led or co-hosted sessions with NGOs, schools, and community groups to increase awareness of emerging threats and reporting processes.

- **Partnership Media Kits**

Communication resources for partner organizations, allowing them to amplify police-led awareness messages through their own channels.

- **Annual Cyber Safety Week**

  A recurring event coordinated by police to highlight prevention messages, share success stories, and promote the victim services package.

By consistently engaging with communities through accessible, relevant, and credible outreach, police can reduce the risk of victimization, increase trust in law enforcement's digital expertise, and ensure that citizens are more likely to report cybercrime promptly and seek help.

The five components of the Comprehensive Victim Services Package provide a practical, scalable, and victim-centered blueprint for police-led cybercrime response. By integrating standardized first-responder tools, clear victim information, structured referral pathways, coordinated case management, and proactive community outreach, law enforcement agencies can transform their role from reactive investigators to proactive partners in recovery. Grounded in the findings from previous chapters and informed by proven international models, this package ensures that every individual who reports a cybercrime receives consistent, timely, and compassionate support, regardless of where they live or their level of digital literacy.

7.5 Implementation Strategy for Police Agencies

The successful adoption of the Comprehensive Victim Services Package requires careful planning, phased integration, and strong leadership within law enforcement agencies. As highlighted in Chap. 5, one of the main challenges in victim service delivery is inconsistency, both in the quality of assistance provided and in the speed of response. This section outlines a practical roadmap for implementing the package across municipal, regional, or national police services, ensuring that the model is operational, sustainable, and adaptable to evolving cybercrime trends [1–4].

In addition, the analysis in Chap. 6 of jurisdictional barriers, resource inequalities, and low reporting rates provides critical lessons for implementation. Cross-border conflicts often delay service restoration, limited resources in certain jurisdictions restrict access to victim support, and underreporting undermines the effectiveness of assistance programs. These international challenges highlight the importance of designing a package that is scalable, resource-sensitive, and capable of fostering public trust. By addressing these issues at the planning stage, the package can achieve greater resilience and ensure equitable access to services, even in resource-constrained environments.

1. Leadership Commitment and Policy Integration

   - Secure senior command endorsement to formally recognize cybercrime victim support as a core policing function.

- Incorporate the package into agency policy, standard operating procedures (SOPs), and officer performance metrics.
- Designate a **Cybercrime Victim Services Lead** within each jurisdiction to oversee implementation.

2. Officer and Staff Training

- Provide **mandatory training modules** on:

  ○ Trauma-informed victim interaction.
  ○ The five service categories from Sect. 7.3.
  ○ Using the First-Responder Toolkit and Case Management Dashboard.

- Include scenario-based exercises for dispatchers, patrol officers, and victim service coordinators.
- Offer periodic refresher courses to address emerging threats and new technology.

3. Technology and Resource Deployment

- Integrate the Case Management Dashboard into existing police records systems.
- Ensure the Referral and Escalation Map and Victim Information Packet are available in both digital and printed formats.
- Provide officers with mobile access to all package resources via secure apps or intranet portals.

4. Partnership Development

- Formalize collaboration agreements with:

  ○ Mental health and crisis support providers.
  ○ Legal aid and advocacy organizations.
  ○ Financial and identity protection services.
  ○ Platform liaison officers for major social media and content-hosting platforms.

- Establish regular multi-agency coordination meetings to review cases, share updates, and refine workflows.

5. Phased Rollout and Pilot Testing

- Begin with a pilot program in select jurisdictions to:

  ○ Test workflows.
  ○ Gather victim feedback.
  ○ Identify resource gaps.

- Use pilot data to adjust protocols before full-scale implementation.
- Roll out nationally in phases, prioritizing areas with higher cybercrime prevalence or resource readiness.

6. Public Awareness and Accessibility
   - Publicize the availability of the package through:
     - Community outreach campaigns.
     - Social media.
     - Partnerships with schools, libraries, and community centers.
   - Provide materials in multiple languages and accessible formats.
7. Monitoring and Continuous Improvement
   - Collect and analyze service delivery metrics (as described in Sect. 7.6).
   - Use victim surveys and case outcome data to refine processes.
   - Stay informed on emerging cyber threats to update toolkit resources and training content.

By embedding this package into operational procedures, police agencies can ensure a consistent, coordinated, and compassionate response to cybercrime victims, building public trust and increasing reporting rates. The implementation strategy prioritizes both operational efficiency and the emotional well-being of victims, creating a model that can be adapted across jurisdictions and sustained over time.

7.6 Key Performance Indicators (KPIs) and Success Metrics

To ensure that the Comprehensive Victim Services Package delivers measurable improvements in victim care and public safety, police agencies must adopt clear, consistent performance indicators. As discussed in Chap. 5, a common weakness of existing victim service frameworks is the absence of systematic monitoring, making it difficult to assess whether victims are receiving timely, effective, and compassionate support. This section outlines KPIs and metrics tailored to law enforcement-led cybercrime victim services, enabling agencies to track impact, identify gaps, and continuously improve delivery.

Insights from Chap. 6 further reinforce the importance of evaluation, as international case studies revealed recurring challenges such as low reporting rates, fragmented service coordination, and insufficient follow-up with victims. By incorporating these lessons into measurable indicators, such as reporting uptake, referral completion, service accessibility, and victim satisfaction, police agencies can ensure that monitoring systems not only capture outputs but also address deeper structural issues identified in global practice.

1. Victim-Centered Outcome Metrics
   - Victim Satisfaction Rate: Percentage of victims rating the police response as satisfactory or higher in post-service surveys.

- Emotional Stabilization Success: Proportion of victims reporting reduced distress after first contact with police.
- Follow-Up Engagement Rate: Percentage of victims who accept and complete at least one referral to support services.

2. Service Delivery Efficiency Metrics

- Time to First Contact: Average time from report submission to initial victim interaction.
- Case Resolution Time: Average duration from first report to case closure or resolution update.
- Referral Completion Rate: Percentage of recommended referrals successfully acted upon by victims.

3. Preventive and Long-Term Impact Metrics

- Repeat Victimization Rate: Percentage of victims experiencing another cybercrime within 12 months.
- Increase in Reporting Rates: Growth in the number of cybercrime cases reported following public awareness of the package.
- Awareness Campaign Reach: Number of people engaged through community outreach and digital awareness programs.

4. Inter-Agency Coordination Metrics

- Multi-Agency Response Time: Average time from referral to partner agency action.
- Joint Case Management Success Rate: Proportion of cases benefiting from coordinated input across police, legal aid, and mental health services.
- Data Sharing Compliance: Adherence to privacy and consent protocols in all cross-agency exchanges.

5. Quality Assurance Metrics

- Adherence to Service Protocols: Proportion of cases in which the First-Responder Toolkit and Referral Map were used as intended.
- Training Completion Rate: Percentage of frontline staff and dispatchers who have completed package-specific training.
- Continuous Improvement Actions Taken: Number of procedural or resource updates made annually based on victim feedback and KPI analysis.

By tracking these metrics regularly, police agencies can maintain accountability, build public trust, and ensure that the package is not only implemented but continually refined. KPI results should be reviewed quarterly and made available in public-facing reports to demonstrate transparency and commitment to victim-centered policing.

7.7 Limitations and Ethical Considerations

While the Comprehensive Victim Services Package offers a structured and scalable approach to supporting cybercrime victims, its implementation within police agencies is subject to several limitations and ethical considerations. As discussed in Chaps. 4 and 5, any victim service model must balance operational feasibility with victim autonomy, privacy, and equity. Recognizing these constraints at the outset will help agencies deploy the package responsibly and sustain public trust.

In addition, Chap. 6 highlighted international concerns about cross-border data sharing, uneven access to victim services, and the risk of secondary victimization in poorly coordinated systems. These lessons underscore the need to integrate strong safeguards into the package, ensuring that victims' rights are protected, that services remain accessible regardless of geography or resources, and that police-led interventions prioritize care and dignity alongside investigative objectives.

1. Resource Constraints

Not all jurisdictions will have the same financial, technical, or human resources to implement every component of the package immediately. Rural or smaller police services may struggle to:

- Maintain trained personnel dedicated to victim services.
- Provide multilingual or culturally adapted materials.
- Integrate advanced tools such as a Case Management Dashboard without significant investment.

Mitigation: Adopt a phased rollout, starting with the most essential components (First-Responder Toolkit, Victim Information Packet) and expand capacity over time.

2. Privacy and Data Protection Risks

Managing sensitive victim information, especially through multi-agency coordination, carries risks of data breaches, unauthorized sharing, or misuse.

- Victims may be reluctant to share information if they fear it could be accessed by unintended parties.
- Cross-border cooperation may involve varying privacy standards.

Mitigation: Implement strict access controls, encryption, and consent-based information sharing in compliance with applicable laws (e.g., GDPR, PIPEDA).

3. Victim Autonomy and Consent

While well-intentioned, proactive referrals and follow-ups can be perceived as intrusive if victims feel pressured.

- Some victims may choose not to engage with certain services or may wish to disengage entirely.
- Over-involvement can inadvertently retraumatize survivors.

Mitigation: Ensure that participation in any service beyond initial police contact is entirely voluntary and based on informed consent.

4. Equity and Accessibility Challenges

As outlined in Chap. 4, marginalized groups, such as seniors, newcomers, and people with disabilities, face additional barriers in accessing victim services.

- A "one-size-fits-all" approach can leave these populations underserved.
- Digital-only delivery of resources may exclude those without reliable internet access.

Mitigation: Provide multiple formats (print, phone-based support, in-person visits) and work with community organizations to tailor resources.

5. Jurisdictional and Legal Limitations

Some cybercrimes, especially those involving international perpetrators, may be beyond the investigative or prosecutorial reach of local police.

- Victims may feel misled if they believe police can guarantee resolution in all cases.
- Legal frameworks may not yet address certain emerging cybercrime types.

Mitigation: Clearly communicate investigative limits while ensuring victims still receive protective, emotional, and advisory support.

6. Maintaining Boundaries of Police Roles

It is essential that police remain facilitators of victim support rather than replacing specialized professionals.

- Officers should not attempt to deliver technical services beyond their expertise.
- Psychological care and legal advice must be referred to qualified providers.

Mitigation: Use the Referral and Escalation Map to ensure victims are guided to the right specialists while police focus on immediate safety, evidence collection, and case coordination.

By acknowledging these limitations and embedding safeguards, police agencies can deploy the package in a manner that is both effective and ethically sound. This awareness ensures that while the service is comprehensive, it remains adaptable, culturally sensitive, and respectful of victim autonomy.

7.8 Chapter Summary

This chapter has translated the analytical insights and case study findings from the previous chapters into a practical, operational framework for police-led cybercrime victim support. The Comprehensive Victim Services Package outlined here is designed to ensure that every individual who contacts law enforcement after experiencing a cyber incident receives consistent, timely, and compassionate assistance, regardless of location, background, or digital literacy level.

By organizing support into five service categories and delivering them through a modular package of toolkits, victim information resources, referral pathways, case management systems, and outreach programs, this model positions police agencies as active partners in victim recovery. The proposed implementation strategy, performance metrics, and ethical safeguards ensure that the package is both actionable and accountable, with built-in mechanisms for continuous improvement.

Grounded in the realities of victim experiences described in Chap. 4, shaped by the legal and policy analysis in Chap. 5, and inspired by effective practices in countries such as Australia, the UK, Canada, and Finland, this package represents a scalable, adaptable solution for modern policing in the digital age. Its adoption would not only improve victim outcomes but also strengthen public trust in law enforcement's ability to respond meaningfully to cyber threats.

The next chapter will build upon this foundation by presenting policy recommendations and long-term strategies to institutionalize victim-centered cybercrime response at national and international levels.

References

1. Australian Cyber Security Centre. (2023). *IDCARE–Australia and New Zealand's national identity & cyber support service*. Australian Government. https://www.idcare.org
2. City of London Police. (2023). *Action Fraud–National fraud & cybercrime reporting centre*. UK Government. https://www.actionfraud.police.uk
3. Royal Canadian Mounted Police. (2023). *RCMP Victim Services–Support for victims of crime*. Government of Canada. https://www.rcmp-grc.gc.ca/en/victims
4. European Union. (2018). *General data protection regulation (GDPR)*, regulation (EU) 2016/679 of the European Parliament and of the council. *Official Journal of the European Union, L, 119*, 1–88. https://eur-lex.europa.eu/eli/reg/2016/679/oj
5. Government of Canada. (2023). *Personal Information Protection and Electronic Documents Act (PIPEDA)*, S.C. 2000, c. 5. Justice Laws Website. https://laws-lois.justice.gc.ca/eng/acts/P-8.6/
6. Finlex. (2023). *Victim support and multi-agency cooperation in Finland*. Ministry of Justice, Finland. https://www.finlex.fi.
7. Royal Canadian Mounted Police. (2023). *Canadian Anti-Fraud Centre (CAFC)*. Government of Canada. https://www.antifraudcentre-centreantifraude.ca
8. Victim Support Finland. (2023). *RIKU–National victim support services*. Victim Support Finland. https://www.riku.fi

Chapter 8
Conclusion

Cybercrime represents a profound evolution in criminal behavior, victimization, and societal harm. As established throughout this book, traditional criminological and victimological frameworks remain highly relevant, but they require careful adaptation to the realities of digital environments. Chapters 1 and 2 outlined this theoretical foundation, demonstrating how concepts such as routine activity theory, social learning, and strain theory can be translated to the online domain, while also emphasizing the psychological, social, and economic dimensions of victimization.

Building on this foundation, Chapters 3 through 5 provided a comparative view of national and regional approaches. Case studies from Australia, Finland, the United Kingdom, and Canada demonstrated the diversity of legal and institutional responses, highlighting both innovative practices, such as Australia's IDCARE, the UK's Action Fraud system, and Finland's multi-agency victim coordination, and persistent limitations in delivering consistent, trauma-informed services. These national insights were further expanded in Chapter 6, which examined the global landscape of victim services. International frameworks such as the Budapest Convention, the UN Cybercrime Convention, and ITU's legislative toolkit illustrate the growing recognition of victim rights, while organizations like Europol's EC3, the Cyber Helpline, and the CyberPeace Institute showcase operational models of support. Yet, fragmentation, jurisdictional barriers, and resource inequalities remain central challenges.

Chapter 7 synthesized these lessons into the proposal for a Comprehensive Cybercrime Victim Services Package, designed for deployment within police agencies. This package represents the core contribution of this work: a victim-centered, modular, and scalable framework that integrates legal, psychological, financial, and technical support into a unified response system. By drawing on both national case studies and international best practices, the package addresses the most pressing gaps identified in earlier chapters, lack of coordination, low reporting rates, uneven quality of service, and inadequate follow-up. At its heart lies a recognition that cybercrime victims experience real harm, and that police institutions must respond with sensitivity, professionalism, and efficiency.

M. K. A. Lukings et al., *Understanding Cybercrime Victim Services*, Progress in IS,
https://doi.org/10.1007/978-3-032-13273-4_8

Taken together, the chapters in this book underscore a central conclusion: victim support is not a peripheral concern in cybercrime policy, but a core component of public safety and digital trust. The proposed package, while ambitious, is grounded in comparative analysis and international best practice, making it both achievable and adaptable.

Looking forward, three priorities emerge. First, policymakers must establish stronger international mechanisms for cross-border victim protection, ensuring that national packages do not operate in isolation. Second, researchers should continue to refine criminological and victimological theories for the digital age, deepening our understanding of how victims experience and respond to cyber harms. Third, police agencies must commit to building cultures of victim-centered practice, integrating the tools, training, and partnerships necessary to make the proposed package sustainable.

In conclusion, this work bridges the gap between theory and practice, between global policy and national implementation, and between fragmented services and an integrated model. By doing so, it lays the groundwork for a future in which cybercrime victims are not left isolated, but are supported through comprehensive, coordinated, and compassionate services.

MIX
Papier aus verantwortungsvollen Quellen
Paper from responsible sources
FSC® C105338

If you have any concerns about our products,
you can contact us on
ProductSafety@springernature.com

In case Publisher is established outside the EU,
the EU authorized representative is:
Springer Nature Customer Service Center GmbH
Europaplatz 3, 69115 Heidelberg, Germany

Printed by Libri Plureos GmbH
in Hamburg, Germany